MW00899460

JUSTICE?
OR JUST US

DAVID AND PENNY PRICE

Copyright © 2019 David and Penny Price
All rights reserved
First Edition

PAGE PUBLISHING, INC.
New York, NY

First originally published by Page Publishing, Inc. 2019

ISBN 978-1-64544-045-1 (Paperback)
ISBN 978-1-64584-569-0 (Hardcover)
ISBN 978-1-64544-046-8 (Digital)

Printed in the United States of America

CONTENTS

PREFACE

David, an all-star athlete from a small Midwestern family dairy farm, develops a major back disability and, in his struggle to adjust, reads his name in the *Milwaukee Journal* newspaper under a two-count federal indictment, facing eighty years in prison without parole and $4 million in fines.

In the meantime, Penny, the cute housewife and mother, contracts cancer. David's incarceration is delayed twice so he can be by her side through radical surgery and radiation treatments. Ultimately, he is sent to a federal prison camp, suffers further injury to his spine, and is transferred to the Federal Medical Center in Rochester, Minnesota. The building he resides in contains mostly old "mobsters." In a short time, he has them drinking hydrogen peroxide for their various illnesses, including cancer, with amazing clinical results, all while learning from an inmate judge (from Chicago) how to write his own pro se appeal. He becomes a jailhouse lawyer who eventually wins his liberty from his illegal sentence only to go home and bury his wife of sixteen years on their daughter's fifteenth birthday. Penny was only thirty-seven years old.

He then files a legal malpractice suit against his lawyer, Gerald P. Boyle, who is busy defending Milwaukee's serial killer Jeffrey Dahmer, *again*! Four and a half years and nine judges later...

Supporting Material

According to the Justice Department's Bureau of Statistics, one in every thirty-seven US adults was either imprisoned at the end of 2001 or had been incarcerated at one time. The study found that 5.6

million, or 2.7 percent of the adult population, have "prison experience." The government study projects that, by 2010, about 3.4 percent of the adult US population will have served time in prison. That translates to about 7.7 million people.

Justice, or Just US? is supported by facts and court documents that will make it a choice for libraries across the land. Our audience is in the six million people caught up in the justice system, and add to that their families, friends, and acquaintances, plus the law professionals, associates, and the curious who want to know what life is like inside a federal prison.

Inside those walls, I taught reading and basic math. As a jailhouse lawyer, I wrote "cop-outs" to the warden, administrative remedies, parole hearing appeals, affidavits, a motion for bail pending appeal, a motion to deny summary judgment, an appeal to the Sixth Circuit Court of Appeals, and more.

This story has many celebrities in it, and the truth shall no longer remain sealed.

I'm interested in your reaction and thoughts to my project.

Respectfully and Sincerely,
David L. Price

Introduction

With my confidence brimming, I make the phone call to the judge's law clerk only to hear, "While the court sympathizes with the plight of Mr. Price's family, there are very few cases where the incarceration of a defendant does not impose a hardship on the family members. The court will deny Mr. Price's motion to reconsider..."

Instantly the telephone beats a hole in the wall as the receiver splits in two. Smoke now billows through the kitchen. The neglected hamburgers are being reduced to char as the frying pan permeates the foul odor of burnt grease. Oh my god, I have to go to *prison*!

The very next day, Penny and Samantha take me to the airport in Milwaukee, with the order from the court fresh in our minds, the ticket clerk is ignorant to the sadness we portray. Samantha, merely twelve years old, never stops crying. I try to reassure her by telling her, "Honey, please don't worry. It'll be all right." Listening to the echoes of my voice, I realize just how feeble I sound. What a lame statement. I'm crying, too, and it's not helping. There is no one here for my wife and child.

It's time to go.

No more passengers are boarding the plane. As I turn back for one last look before I disappear into the bowels of the plane, Samantha drapes herself over her mother.

No words can describe the grief and sadness that pervaded the air. The most difficult goodbye I will ever do. Or so I thought. As I walk through the tunnel, it feels like a giant rubber band is harnessed to my back. Each step becomes harder, and like a pulling horse, I'm struggling with each step.

Suddenly the rubber band of freedom snaps and the door shuts. I'm in a trance. Am I dreaming a nightmare? My eyes remain fixed out the plane's small window. Oblivious to any passengers, I stare at the retreating hangar behind a wall of tears.

My seat belt secured, eyes closed, and head back, I can hear Dad getting up and dressing for work...

* * * * *

It was 4:30 a.m. He allowed my two brothers and me the next thirty minutes to remain snuggled and cozy under the quilt that was hand-stitched by Grandma years ago, before he telephoned from the barn. When the phone rang from the barn at 5:00 a.m., it was chore time. Gary would carry the milk in half-filled pails to the milk house and step up onto the plank that was laid over a pair of cement blocks. This provided him the height he needed in order to pour the milk into the strainer without spilling. It was Danny's turn to remove the uneaten hay from the mangers and give it to the young stock waiting in the barnyard, my turn to climb the silo and fork down enough silage. It was always a dark climb, and my eyes would adjust like an owl's, and when the sun rose, it would seem as if God's light bulb was once again on. Careful not to dig holes, which invited mold, I'd throw down enough corn silage for forty cows, which Danny would feed. It was my job to run the barn cleaner into the spreader while Dad and Gary finished up the milking, and Danny the feeding. As I spread the manure in the designated field, Gary fed the baby calves and Danny would help Dad wash up the milk house. Not until chores were done could the three of us go to the house, eat, and get ready for the school bus, which always arrived at 7:10 a.m. sharp.

This was an everyday protocol, for we lived and played on the family farm. The 1950s countryside was sprinkled with small family farms like ours, with hay forts in the haymow, a treehouse in the yard, dogs running free—no leashes—and neighbors helping neighbors no matter what the task might be.

I shall always be a farm kid at heart.

As a high school senior in 1970, I was voted president of the FFA (Future Farmers of America), repeated as most valuable wrestler, and received the National W Award for my achievements in scholastics and sports. As much as farming was my life, it wasn't to be. Our family had grown to ten children. Gary was now married and a butcher at the local meat market. Danny went to town and got a job working in manufacturing. Later on, he bought a sports car and reveled in the fact that he had weekends off and more money. I left to spend time with the United States Marine Corps.

God sent me an angel

Returning home, I met, became friends, fell in love, got married, and settled down with one of the most wonderful women God ever created. Life was great. My work took me too into manufacturing and meat-cutting. I loved being a husband and a father. In 1976, when we were in our first year of marriage, you could find Penny in front of the television, watching the Milwaukee bowling show, *Scotch 300 Doubles*. It was on every weekday at 11:30 a.m., and Penny never missed a day.

Who wants to bowl a game?

"Come on! Let's try out for it. It'll be fun!" Her voice burst with excitement as she served supper.

How could I resist? I had never seen the show, thanks to my first-shift job, but I said yes. After all, she was the bowler in the family.

In the late 1950s, when Penny wasn't much taller than the ball racks, her parents installed Brunswick automatic pinsetters in their twelve-lane bowling alley. If you wanted to find Penny, you just looked past the ball racks. This short little "tomboy" with silky hair and the round Shirley Temple face complete with Danish red freckles would always be hustling somebody for a game. Usually, it was somebody from one of the three bars inside the supper club that was also part of her parents' establishment. But they were never any match for Penny.

To watch her bowl was like watching a professional. Her five-step delivery was quick. Her release, smooth and silent, sent the ball down the lane on a cushion of air straight to the "pocket." She commanded control. If she needed three strikes in the tenth frame, she got 'em!

One evening, the place was packed with as many spectators as bowlers. It was league time in America's most popular participating leisure sport. The humming from the balls traveling down the lanes was interrupted with the banging of pins. Laughter, cheering, and the aroma of tobacco and alcohol were evidence of people having a good time.

Soon the sound began to taper off. All was silent. Everyone had stopped bowling, and a crowd gathered behind lane 6. Penny was the only one still bowling. Eleven strikes in a row! Wow! You could hear whispering, but you could not hear the ball hit her lane until it thundered through the pins, and when it was over, not even the roar of the crowd could convince the defiant ten-pin to do anything more than wiggle.

We bowled in Milwaukee's televised tournament and won round 1, one hundred silver dollars and a return trip for round 2. We began the next round with Penny nervously hiding behind her hand as she bit down hard on her fingernails. It didn't help when I ordered a drink from the bar and dropped it all across the alley in front of the foul line. Penny and the contestants stood perfectly still, not taking a step, until the lane was completely dry.

I was embarrassed.

* * * * *

Penny and David Price Win $1,000 in
Bowling Tourney in Milwaukee

Penny and David Price entered their first bowling tournament on July 24 and, on August 9, were awarded the first-place grand championship.

The *Scotch 300 Doubles* tournament was sponsored by WTMJ Channel 4, Milwaukee, and was held at Red Carpet Lanes Bowlero in Wauwatosa.

The couple tried out for qualifications on July 24, a Sunday morning, at 7:00 a.m., and qualified

11

with a 508 series. That score seeded them in first place for round 1 on July 28, a Thursday night.

Round 1 began taping for television at 6:00 p.m., and at 7:00 p.m., David and Penny had won their first game with a score of 233. That victory put them in competition with all other first-place daily winners. Having a score of 233 seeded them in second place for round 2. Their first match of round 2 was another victory with a high game of 253. Winning that game allowed Dave and Penny to bowl against the couple seeded first. It was another win for the Prices when they scored with a 225 game. That was the key victory winning them one hundred silver dollars and enabling them to return for the championship qualifications round.

On Saturday, August 6, at 1:00 p.m., Penny and Dave returned to Bowlero and bowled a 501 series. It was at this point they had made the semifinals.

The semifinals and finals were on August 9, Tuesday. Dave and Penny were seeded in second place and scheduled to bowl at 3:30 p.m. Their first game was a must and so be it with another victory of 191. Now it was the last game of the semifinals, and they were up against the number 1 couple of twenty finalists. The first-place couple was a brother and sister from Lake Geneva. It was only a reality when, in the end of the tenth frame, the scores read 226 to 181 in favor of Penny and David Price. That was the semifinals, and at 7:00 p.m., the finals began with Penny and Dave seeded first, with only one more game to go. They turned a dream full of hopes into a first-place grand championship, bowling a 218 and winning a check for $1,000.

You can watch the whole tournament on Penny and Dave on Channel 4 WTMJ television at the following times:

August 18, 11:30 a.m. to 12 noon
August 19, 11:30 a.m. to 12 noon
September 12, 11:30 a.m. to 12 noon
September 16, 11:30 a.m. to 12 noon

David and Penny are most grateful to Mr. and Mrs. Don Oberholtzer and family, Mrs. Evelyn Oberholtzer, Mr. and Mrs. Robert Price and family, Leeshore Supper Club and Lanes, and Alby Materials Inc. for their efforts in helping them bring home the championship.

When it is over, our dreams turn into reality when we win the first-place grand championship: a check for $1,000!

The sponsor hands the check to Penny, and the announcer asks, "What are you going to do with all that money?" Being a young wife and mother, she answers, "We have a little girl, and she would like some toys!"

We decided to take a vacation to Canada with my brother Carl and his girlfriend, Joey.

The roof rack is loaded and tied down, the trunk is packed with camping gear, and the old Chrysler, with its four passengers, continues to chug its way along the gravel road north toward Hudson Bay. Suddenly without warning, the steering wheel jerks violently back and forth. Carl brings the car to a halt with the right front tire flat.

Penny and Joey both say, "We knew this was a bad idea!" My reassuring them, "Not to worry," doesn't help when they realize that neither my brother Carl nor I can get the tire's lug nuts loose. Carl is a tall, very powerfully built athletic-type who spends much of his spare time lifting weights. And he can't do it!

My turn. Yes, the angled tire wrench keeps slipping off the lug nuts and is now beginning to round the edges off. If we keep this up, the nuts will be so badly damaged we'll never get anywhere. Perhaps the proper wrench, the one shaped like a cross, will give us the perpendicular leverage to loosen the nuts instead of the one-sided angle wrench that comes with the car.

Penny, who possesses a huge vocabulary, is beginning to turn her fears into a panic attack with a constant barrage of "How come..." and "What if..." Joey, on the other hand, is shy and quietly withdraws to the back seat to start crying. Carl's reaction to the frustration turns into anger with fits of violent outbursts, banging, punching, and kicking the car.

"Hold it. Everybody quiet down. This isn't going to solve our problem," I say, but even I am scared.

We have been traveling this desolate road for hours and haven't seen one vehicle, and we have been stranded since the middle of the afternoon and darkness is approaching and there is still no traffic.

Since it has been my idea to abandon the original camping route around Lake Superior and go exploring, I accept the blame for being stranded and volunteer to start walking at dawn's first light. In the meantime, everyone settles in for a night in the car.

Sometime after midnight, lights appear in the far, distant north, and we hear the growling of a giant road grader. As the huge machine comes to a stop next to us, the smell of diesel fuel and dust penetrates the car. Stepping out of the car, I notice the machine's tires are taller than the car's open door. Nevertheless, I reach up to grab the ladder railing, only to feel the vibration of power from the idling machine.

Inside the cab, a small gray-haired man with a long black handlebar mustache asks, "You guys all right?" I quickly explain our problem with the tire iron. Swiftly he responds, "Get in. I'll take you down by my son. He'll help you." The old man and I immediately drive off, grading the road as we leave, despite my not explaining to the ladies the grader man's plan. Carl remains with the ladies, who anxiously anticipate my return.

I watch the car disappear into the distant darkness while the old man talks. "I'm going to let you out at the side road leading to the logging camp. Follow the road until you come to a fork. Take the road to the right until you see a yard light. There will be a group of three buildings. Go into the center building. Inside to your left is a stairway. Upstairs is my son's room, the second one on your left. Wake him up and he'll help you."

Climbing out of the cab, I meekly ask, "Can't you give me a ride?"

He replies, "The company pays me too much money to be a taxi."

I thank him and stand in the moonlit darkness. I tell myself silently, *Get a grip!* Grass grows down the center of the road I am on.

I look up, and the stars look inches from the treetops. The timber along the road appears to swallow up the trail before me. I can't see, but my hearing is more than making up for my optical impairment. I can hear water tumbling and splashing off rocks just through the trees to my left. A branch snaps to my right. A deer? Or something else?

Following the instructions, I walk. Suddenly, out of the darkness, from behind the trees toward the river comes a soft grunt. Fear makes the hair on the back of my neck stand up. Now a long growl and the sound of breaking branches. *Oh, no, a bear!* Running with the speed of a frightened gazelle, I scurry for the safety of the logging camp. Soon the yard light comes into view, then the three buildings to the right, as the grader man said.

Jogging now to catch my breath, I dart into the middle building and see 4:00 a.m. on the hallway clock. Up the stairs I go, stopping at the second door on the left, knocking three times, only to find a silent response. Again, only louder. This time, a sleepy reply.

"Who is it?"

Courageously I answer, "It's me, Dave. I'm from the United States, and I have a flat tire."

A long moment of silence is followed with a very loud "WHAT?"

I quickly explain before the door opens, "Your dad picked me up while he was grading. I don't have the right wrench, and he said you would help me."

The door opens. A groggy young man introduces himself as Mark.

We drive to the stranded vehicle, and Mark announces, "This is a Chrysler! You don't need my tire wrench. The right-side tires have opposite threads!"

Astonished, embarrassed, and grateful, I ask Mark, "Do you want a beer?"

Humbled, we make it back home in time for our pool league awards banquet. We take first place shooting for Penny's father. He owns Obie's Cobblestone, a three-story cobblestone hotel originally named Buena Vista. It comes with a rich history dating back to 1844. Abraham Lincoln slept here when he was campaigning to be president. The building is also listed on the National Register of Historic Places.

**OBIE'S COBBLESTONE
BAR & RESTAURANT**
East Troy, Wis.

The team and I party till closing. In the midst of our party, the subject of the famous Lapham Peak dare comes up. With my confidence inflated by alcohol, I courageously and foolishly accept.

Two carloads of witnesses escort me to the park. It's 2:30 a.m., and there is no backing down. I stand on the top of the hill, a brisk, icy breeze cutting through my jacket, rattling my bones with its chill. The stars twinkle over my head while the moon lays out her brightest rays of light.

There it is, a huge, towering metal ladder surrounded by three tubular legs supported by nine cable-thin arms that reach down and grab ahold of the earth so the tall metal body can stand erect.

I reach out and feel the bite of cold steel on my bare hands. Giving the top a second look, I decide to penetrate the darkness, scaling all of the tower's 360 feet. Up and up I climb, hand over hand, foot over foot, working my way skyward. I will not look down until I get to the top, I decide. Nearing the tops of the trees, which surround me like stationary soldiers, I begin to feel the excessive pressure of the east wind that wants me off the tower. I continue my ascent anyway. Coming to the first set of three support cables, I encounter three giant drums positioned so that each looks away from the other. Climbing between them, I hide from my enemy, the wind.

As I look up toward the top, the ladder continues upward until it runs out of sight, like looking up railroad tracks that carry you off into the distance. Thinking only about the top, I climb on. As I reach the second set of guy cables, I realize two-thirds of my goal; however, I am experiencing something I have not taken into consideration—the power of the wind wearing down my muscles to the point of exhaustion and failure.

An ache in my forearms turns into a blaze of pain. Hot fire runs through my veins, trying to tell my brain, "Enough!" But I don't listen. I can't listen. All I can think of is my goal, the top of the highest tower on the highest hill in Southeastern Wisconsin! Suddenly, the paralyzing numbness of a cramp cripples my fingers, coiling them shut. As I quickly stick my arms through the ladder and grab ahold of the next rung with my elbow joint, thoughts race through my head. *Can I hang on? Am I going to fall? What is Penny going to think?*

Focusing my attention on my goal, I realize I'm three-quarters of the way there. With my hands cramping up, going back down is out of the question. I must go up—it is shorter than going down. So with ray elbows for hands, I continue on up. Fear begins to overcome me now. Shaking with panic, I understand that my only way out is up to the top so I can rest on the perch. The wind becomes more vicious with each rung of the ladder. Looking up, I count each of the seven rungs to go. Slowly, one arm at a time, I put each one through up to the crook of my elbow, not caring how sore the skin on the inside of my arms is becoming. Then like a blast from the back of a jet engine, the wind begins to scream. I fight with all the strength I have left, and my fear turns into panic as my biceps begin to cramp and coil into hard knots. Crying, I beg God for the strength to continue. I look up: only three rungs remain. With hands crippled with cramps and arms that no longer can straighten, I force myself up. Only two left. I must continue. Fear and anger compel me to endure the pain one more time. As I position myself on the tower, I realize two things: One, I've made it. Two, I have to climb back down.

With my eyes finally opening and the pain of overworked muscles receding, I turn my attention to the view. To the east, down under my feet lie over one million people quietly sleeping beneath the twinkling blanket of Milwaukee's lights. Beyond the glimmering lights of the city stretches Lake Michigan. Slightly to my left, I feel as if I can reach out and touch the magnificent Catholic church at the top of Holy Hill. Beyond that, the city called West Bend reflects its lights as a short white line on the horizon to the northeast. To the north, the glow reflecting itself off the low-floating night clouds stretching long and flat must be Beaver Dam. Behind me lie Oconomowoc, Watertown, Whitewater, and all the small towns in between. Nobody can see what I'm seeing unless they are flying.

Resting on the perch, I study the landscape. With dawn's light fast approaching, I notice that the tower's hill is centered in a glacial drumlin, an oval range of hills that jut up over the otherwise flat land that gradually inclines toward Lake Michigan, similar to a mountain range sticking up over the prairie.

Looking back, I follow the expressway west toward Madison as it threads its way between lakes and cities. I cannot believe all the lakes I can see—Okauchee, Pewaukee, Oconomowoc—spilling their way into the Fox River. I follow the river south and pick up the waters of Beulah, Eagle, Upper and Lower Phantom, Lauderdale, Pleasant, Pickerel, Swift, Booth, Army, Potters, Tichigan, and Muskego Lakes, as if denying the presence of Lake Michigan and going south to Illinois instead. I'm high. Too high.

As I look east again over the top of Milwaukee, Lake Michigan's water reflects the transformation of colors along the edge of the darkened sky. A fire begins to stretch out before me on the blue horizon below. Stars fade, while behind me, the darkness leaves, taking with it my umbrella of stars. Casting away their gray shadows, clouds awaken with red, pink, and orange.

The sun appears, bringing warmth to my body, so I no longer shake from the cold of the night or from the terror and fright that comes with such a height. With the wind in my face and the earth at my feet, I can feel the Earth's rotation, like a descending chair on a Ferris wheel, toward the sun.

As I look down, I see two Waukesha County police cars traveling south on HWY 83. Sure enough, they continue on my path. They turn right on HWY 18, then another right on County Road C. And as if I left a trail of bread crumbs right to me, they follow County Road C for a mile, turn right onto Lapham Peak Road, and park right under my tower.

Holding my arm extended straight down, I can cover both paddy wagons with my thumbnail. As for coming down, they are going to have to wait.

It is shortly after sunrise when the police arrive. By the time I finally make it to the ground, it is 9:30 a.m., much to the cheers of the partying spectators. A trip to the jail follows, with a $50 trespassing fine.

I will never climb another tower again.

Chapter 1

The Tragedy

A few years later, in 1979, knowing blue is Penny's favorite color, I secretly purchase a brand-new Pontiac Grand Prix and tape the keys inside her Mother's Day card. At this time, $11,000 isn't even a third of my annual income. Life is as good as it can get.

Then disaster strikes. My older brother, Gary, is killed on the job. He has always been my best friend. I am diagnosed as having a degenerative spinal disease. My life of holding down two jobs, earning over $34,000 a year, which permits Penny to stay home and be a bowler and a mother to our daughter, is over. A fact that I have trouble accepting. At this time, I refuse to admit there is anything wrong with my back. Denial is strong. It costs me my job and leads me to see Dr. Paul Sydman, a psychologist, who makes me realize I need medical treatment and to accept it. But not until we suffer through bankruptcy, eviction, and moving in with relatives.

I volunteer for an experimental treatment at University Hospital in Madison. They inject a meat tenderizer (chymopapain) into my ruptured disk, which is supposed to dissolve it. I end up in a wheelchair, paralyzed from the waist down. My spirit now rests on the clouds of hopelessness and despair. It doesn't seem fair. After all, I am the second eldest of the seven Price brothers, who are the "winningest" family in the history of Wisconsin High School wrestling! Seeing life from a wheelchair, I watch my youngest brother, Ted, win the 167-pound state championship, finishing the twenty-year dynasty of the seven Price boys, with an undefeated (32-0) season. Ted later goes on to college and becomes an NCAA II champion as a junior and runner-up as a senior.

In March of 1985, I undergo major back surgery; however, the surgeons are not able to correct the 50 percent slippage of the L-4 on L-5 vertebrae, so they stabilize it by wiring in a metal bracket and fusing three of my lumbar vertebrae with bone carved from my hip.

The following years of therapy are very difficult both physically and emotionally. The fact that I am no longer able to be the person I grew up as is extremely hard to accept.

I now become involved with the Department of Vocational Rehabilitation (DVR), going to school at Waukesha County Technical Institute (WCTI) in Pewaukee, learning electronics. My grade point for the summer and fall semester is a 4.0. However, on the first day of the second semester, en route to school, Penny and I are in an auto accident that totals our car and aggravates my back. I can no longer attend school.

Penny now works two jobs to support our little family and keep us ahead of the accumulating medical bills that are suffocating us. My parents get back their farm because the man they've sold it to goes bankrupt and they let us move into the house so we can move out of my brother-in-law's home. Being disabled is taking its toll on me. Penny is now the provider and I am not adjusting to the role of Mr. Mom. Many of the duties of the house will throw out my back, like getting the milk out of the refrigerator, pulling down the window shade, vacuuming, putting the dishes away, and making the bed, reminding me constantly, when I least expect it, that I am never going to be the same again.

It is at this time, against my better judgment, that I start drinking alcohol. It isn't a lot at first, but after a while, I begin to hide booze around the house and drink at all hours of the day in secret. As a drunkard, I find it easy to get involved with drugs. By the grace of God and the love from Penny, I enter into Kettle Morain Hospital on January 8, 1988, and sober up. Thirty days later, I am released.

My aftercare program is going to Alcoholics Anonymous (AA). They help me accept the fact of who I now am, let go of my anger, and stop feeling sorry for myself. At the weekly AA meetings, I always introduce myself as "David, I am a drug addict, and my choice of drug is alcohol." This doesn't sit well with the older ones, and instead of focusing on the issues, we spend too much time debating if alcohol is a drug or not. Eventually, I stay home.

With the speculation of making money, I let myself be persuaded into getting involved with growing marijuana. In the months that follow, I have a hard time accepting what I am doing. So it comes to pass on August 10, 1988, that I am arrested in connection with the seizure of 162 marijuana plants still in the field. The state and local authorities play the battle cry for the "War on Drugs!" in the newspapers. It is election time, and the local district attorney has a field day.

Dean Clinic
1313 Fish Hatchery Road
Madison, WI 53715
(608) 252-8000
August 27, 1988

Ms. Penny Price
Rt. 3, Box 156
Elkhorn, WI 53121
DMC #01/280172.8

Dear Penny:

You need to have your Pap smear repeated. The one performed on August 23 was read as favor for a few mild atypical cells. Essentially, what this means is that the person who is the cytologist had difficulty reading the slide. In no way is this suggestive of a cancer of the cervix. We need to get another smear.

Sincerely,
Karl A. Rudat, MD
Obstetrics and Gynecology
KAR/BJF

Senior Judge John W. Reynolds
January 11, 1989

David L. Price
Docket No. 88-CR-115
Addendum to Presentence Report

The probation officer certifies that the presentence report, including any revision thereof,
has been made available to the defendant's attorney, counsel for the government, and that the
content of the addendum has been communi-
cated to counsel. The addendum fairly states any
objections they have made.

Objections

By the Government
The probation office has received no objections from the government.

By the Defendant

The defendant, through counsel, raises the following objections. They are summarized as follows:
   Page 7, paragraph 5. The defendant objects
to the statement indicating he leases the property
from Mr. Atkinson. Mr. Price wants it made clear
he only leases the farmhouse and not any land.
   Page 7, paragraph 5. The defendant reports
there is no Highway 9. He states the road specified in the report is actually Highway D.
   Page 11, paragraph 36. The presentence
report inaccurately reports Mr. Price as having
been born in the house he is renting from Mr.

Atkinson. He states he was only raised in this house from the age of twelve. He was actually born in a house on Potters Road in Walworth County.

Page 7, paragraph 5. The defendant and counsel want the court to be made aware that they do not disagree with the amount of marijuana specified in the government's version of the presentence report. However, they do disagree that all this marijuana was a usable product and could be sold as such. The defendant, through counsel, contends the amount of marijuana the government specifies in their version contains a large amount of unusable product, such as stalks and stems. They are hoping the court will take this into consideration at the time or sentencing.

Probation Officer's Response

Regarding the first three objections raised by the defendant, a finding for or against the defendant can have no effect on the application of the guidelines in this case. Regarding the amount of marijuana raised by the defendant, the government advises the amount specified in their version was processed and accurately reflects the totality of the defendant's offense behavior.

Respectfully submitted,
Jerald H. Husz
US Probation Officer

Reviewed and Approved:
Trudi A. Schmitt
Chief U.S. Probation Officer
JHH/dlw

University of Wisconsin–Madison
Medical School
March 27, 1989

To whom it may concern:
Re: Penny Price

This patient was referred to University of
Wisconsin Hospital because of a stage 1B squa-
mous cell carcinoma of the cervix. Following her
workup, there was no evidence of metastatic disease. The patient subsequently had a radical hys-
terectomy and bilateral pelvic lymphadenectomy.
Frozen section at the time of surgery revealed no
disease outside of the cervix. Following surgery,
the pathology report reveals malignant cells in
the pelvic lymph nodes and in the vaginal lym-
phatics. This type of report decreases the patient's
chance of cure significantly.

In an attempt to still cure this patient, I
feel she now needs external radiation therapy
to the pelvis for six to seven weeks, followed by
intracavitary irradiation. Obviously, this patient
is under considerable emotional stress, and any
family support is extremely important.

If there is any additional information you
need, please feel free to contact me.

Sincerely,

Dolores A. Buchler, MD
Professor of
Gynecology and Human Oncology
DAB: rao

United States District Court
Eastern District of Wisconsin

Order
Case No. 88-CR-115

United States of America,
Plaintiff,
Vs.
David L. Price,
Defendant.

Defendant David L. Price has moved for an order staying his prison sentence, or in the alternative, extending the time to surrender for an additional sixty (60) days. Defendant has made this request because his wife is presently undergoing chemotherapy after surgery for cancer of the cervix. The government has not opposed defendant's motion, and the probation department has recommended extending defendant's surrender date to June 23, 1989. The court will, therefore, grant defendant's request to extend his surrender date to June 23, 1989.

It is therefore ordered that defendant David L. Price's present surrender date of April 23, 1989, is extended to June 23, 1989.

Dated at Milwaukee, Wisconsin, this day of April 1989.

By the Court:
John W. Reynolds
Senior Judge

September 1, the federal government gets into the act, and it isn't until Penny comes crying toward me, holding the morning *Milwaukee Sentinel* newspaper, that I learn a federal grand jury has issued a two-count federal indictment against me! The article goes on to mention a ton of marijuana, and I am facing eighty years in prison with no parole and four million dollars in fines. The government should not be allowed to print such exaggerations.

At the time of the arrest and subsequent proceedings, Penny becomes very sick. She passes it off as just her nerves. Besides, she has received an August 27 letter from her doctor that said, "The cytologist had difficulty reading the slide. In no way is this suggestive of a cancer…"

I blame myself for her suffering.

My only trouble with the law thus far was climbing that tower. Now, on January 12, 1989, I stand before the federal district judge, the Honorable John W. Reynolds (former Governor of Wisconsin), senior judge for the Eastern District of Wisconsin, to be sentenced under the US Sentencing Commission Guidelines. The severity of the offense, according to the government, is calculated on the basis of the weight of the plants seized on August 10, which the government calculates to be 340 pounds of marijuana. Nowhere near a ton. Under the guidelines, 340 pounds yielded a range of fifty-one to sixty-three months. I receive fifty-one months. I have thirty days to "get my affairs in order," then voluntarily report to the federal prison camp in Duluth, Minnesota.

I witness true fear and sadness. The enormity of my going to prison for more than four years takes its toll on Penny. The reality of separation is only days away when, on February 6 (Penny's birthday), an 8:00 p.m. phone call comes from her doctor. He says, "Penny has invasive cancer and needs an operation right away!" I am given a sixty-day stay by the court to be with her as she goes through a frightening seven-and-a-half-hour radical surgery to remove the cancer.

On an evening when Penny's visitors have all gone home, the doctor comes to her and explains that the surgery is unsuccessful. The pathology report states the presence of cancer in her lymph glands.

If she wants a priest, they will send one up and leave a sedative with the nurse if she needs it.

Our nightmare is only beginning.

The court grants me another sixty-day stay so I can take her to daily radiation treatments. After forty-two sessions of her being burned by their big machine, the doctor says, "There is nothing more we can do except regular check-ups for the presence of an active tumor and keep her comfortable with drugs when the end comes."

My stomach feels like the bully doctor has just punched the air out of me. I can't breathe. The oncologist walks me to the end of the hallway, where a little makeshift lounge with a couple of chairs, a couch, a TV, and the usual magazines are. I am still standing, supported by Penny's mom and dad, and the doctor continues his assault on Penny's health.

"And 60 percent will redevelop tumors within two years, and she won't be out of the woods for five years."

Trying to make sense of what I'm hearing, I ask, "What are you saying?"

The doctor turns to walk away, but not before answering my question with, "I'm sorry."

"That's it? Sorry?" I reply, clenching my fists. If hitting the doctor will change things, I'm prepared.

Obie, Penny's dad, steps in to reassure me. "Don't worry, Penny is a fighter. She'll beat this. You'll see."

Wow!

I love Penny with all my heart. The pain and suffering she is going through are more than I can bear. Our little Sammie is losing me to prison, and the fear she has for her mother literally breaks my heart. I'm not going to give in or up, and neither is Penny.

I plead with my lawyer, Gerald P. Boyle, "Help me stay my sentence. Get me a lifetime of probation. If I ever break the law again, including a traffic ticket, you can lock me up and throw away the key!"

He responds, "So sad. Too bad. Lots of inmates have relatives that die while they're in prison. I suggest you write to the judge. Besides, you still owe me $9,000!"

Penny cries all the way home.

Dear Judge John W. Reynolds:

I am writing this letter to you concerning your sentencing of my husband, David Price.

Back in January of this year, you made the decision to have David incarcerated for four years and three months in Federal prison. You made that decision from information of his involvement with a conspiracy to manufacture marijuana. Not at that time, or now, do I believe the sentencing was fair or just to fit the crime.

However, I am appealing to you once again for a sincere reconsideration of that sentence. I know that you are aware of the dramatic events that have taken place since February. I have been diagnosed with cancer, have undergone radical surgery, and have gone through seven weeks of intense radiation, and yet another hospital stay.

You were kind enough to provide David with extensions so he could be by my side throughout my medical treatment and I am truly grateful for that.

This letter is a compassionate plea for your reconsideration to enable an honest man to remain with his family. My doctors inform me I am not out of the woods for a five-year period. Presently, there are scheduled physician appointments every three months for the next five years. At this stage of my health, my emotional state is a key factor for my recovery and well-being.

I am asking you to consider the whole picture and the lives affected by a sentence of four years and three months. Please analyze the character of David. His honesty is so much of who he is. If you evaluate the report on David's case, you will see that from the very beginning, he agreed to give his full cooperation. He told the truth. He came forward on his own. He showed the authorities the specific fields where the marijuana was growing, and he testified to the fact that he was glad it was found, that it was a load off his shoulders. He admitted to his involvement and showed only remorse for his mistake. I can tell you in all honesty that the planting of those seeds was for a financial survival of the family. Not a profitable lifestyle of luxury or fast living. It was an attempt to save the family farm and provide food and shelter for the family he so loves. Both David and I acknowledge that what he did was wrong and there should be some sort of punishment. But to take this unselfish, loving man away from his family and destroy the security and foundation of a close family unit does *not* seem to me to be a requisite for justice. I need my husband! I need him to help me make this a better place for our daughter. I can't do it alone.

Judge Reynolds, I am praying that you will take all the circumstances in this situation and reconsider what good David's being incarcerated for four years and three months will do as compared to the bad it will do. I believe there are more benefits to society as well as our own personal family that can be enhanced from David's freedom. He is an excellent teacher, and he can help educate and advance this civilization to a world free of drugs.

I know deep down in my heart you have the power to make this bad situation turned into something of value. I have confidence you will reconsider the original sentence and provide real justice. I believe in you, Judge Reynolds, and I have faith in your help.

God bless you always!

Penny A. Price
Loving Wife of David Price

Like the wicked witch, the halls of justice turn our days into grains of sand sifting through the hourglass of freedom. The sand is just about gone when Penny and I hand-deliver our reconsideration letters to the trust in the court, but our faith is in God, the Lord Almighty, the Help in Peril, the Self-Subsisting. I'm not going to be separated from my wife, my best friend, Samantha's mother, my bowling partner, my card partner, and most importantly, my soul mate. I can still hear her doctor's voice.

"I'm sorry, the surgery was unsuccessful. We took eleven lymph nodes from Penny's pelvis. The pathologist reports four were positive for cancer. We'll monitor her every three months for the presence of an active tumor and keep her comfortable with drugs when the end comes."

When the end comes! I refuse to comprehend those words. I'm only fighting a prison sentence, while Penny battles a death sentence!

I can feel a hand on my shoulder. The soft voice of the stewardess says, "Sir, please fasten your seat belt. We'll be landing soon."

CHAPTER 2

Federal Prison Camp, Duluth

As I descend into Duluth, Minnesota, the ravages of the iron ore industry become visible. The land below is left looking like a bombed-out battlefield, with craters that look like they belong on the moon. I've always pictured prison with walls, armed guards in towers, rolls of razor wire and, tattooed inmates. Federal Prison Camp, Duluth, doesn't need walls and wire. Its remote location on the end of Lake Superior and the forest and swamp leave me feeling I'm somewhere other than Earth.

I still want to run away, but where will I go? I can't go home, where I'm needed. I'll just be found, caught, and punished with more time. Time, ironic as it seems, I don't want, but Penny is fighting for more of. Will cancer claim her before I get out? How can she possibly drive over eight hours to visit me?

The concrete walls are bare and cold, just like my shivering body standing before the guard. "Bend over and spread 'em," he orders. The twelve-inch scar down my spine draws his attention. "What's this about?" he asks.

"I'm disabled with a broken back," I reply.

"Too bad. This is a work camp. Everybody here has gotta work, and that means you too. Now, put your clothes in this box. We'll mail 'em home to your mama. Put these on. Hurry up. Gotta get your mug shot. Here, hold your numbers up. Higher, goddamn it! You're not the only one in here." *Flash.* "Now, move on to clothing."

Lake Superior refrigerates the June air.
An inmate working at clothing asks, "What cha in for?"
"Growing pot," I reply.
"How much time?"
"Fifty-one months."
"How much pot?"
"Ah, 162 plants."
"That's all? No other charges?"
"None."
"He's cool. Can't be a 'rat' with that much time," says the older, hippie-looking inmate with wire-rim glasses. He hands me a coat, a worn-out, faded Army jacket with tattered sleeves.
"Can I have a new one?" I ask.
"New ones are for 'rats,'" explains the first inmate.
I ask him, "What are you in here for?"
"Cocaine," he answers.
"How much time did you get?"

"A nickel."

The older, hippie-looking inmate, handing me size 10.5 boots, says, "I won't pay taxes to the federal government. I had an apple farm in Michigan. I lost it after three bad years in a row. They charged me with 'willful failure to file a return and tax fraud.' I was getting other people to do the same. I don't recommend pissing off the government. Don't ask me how much time I got. Just know that I'll still be here after you go home."

I'm directed to the Douglas unit. It's an old wooden Army barracks. My new home is a four-man room. To the left of the opening is a bunk bed, then a desk and chair, and another bunk bed. Four lockers stand as sentries on the right wall. This is not home. This is a cold existence you can never warm up to. Home is Penny and Sam. I'm holding on tight to the memories of their warm love and laughter.

I'm not here to make friends; I just want to be left alone to protect my memories. I don't want to hear "Why you here?" "How much time?" "How rich were you?" or "How innocent are you?" Go away! Just leave me alone.

The language I hear is disgusting. The words they speak are as foul as this place. I hate this place.

Intake screening, paperwork. Orientation, paperwork. Lecture, paperwork. Medical exam, paperwork. Another lecture, more paperwork.

I've been here two days, with 1,548 more to go. And today is my birthday. Well, happy fucking birthday. I bury my face in my pillow to hide the sobs, and the pillowcase soaks up the tears. My life is torn and shredded, like the Army jacket I wear to keep Lake Superior's breath off me.

Climbing into the top bunk is a drag. There is no ladder. I ask my cellmate, "How do you get a bottom bunk?"

He responds, "Forget about it. You have to be here a while to get a bottom. It's a seniority thing. They assign you a job?"

"No."

"Get that taken care of."

I'm standing in the hallway just outside the unit manager's office. I can hear my counselor, Janet Strombeck, talking. I hate her as much as she hates me. She says, "Price has a bitter attitude and is reluctant to accept staff authority."

"Excuse me?" I interrupt.

"Can we help you?"

"Yeah, I need the form for getting a job."

"It's called inmate request to staff," snips my counselor.

"Whatever!"

"You better change your attitude around here," warns the unit manager.

"Right."

Inmate Request to Staff Member

To: Mr. Dennis Miller, Director of Education

Subject: I believe my five years of math (algebra, geometry, trigonometry, advanced algebra, and calculus) may be of help in assisting inmates with basic math. Calculus was taken in vocational school (4.0).

Disposition: Please assign to "Education."

Dennis Miller
7-7-89

* * * * *

A blackboard exhales chalk dust into the gloomy, dank air, while black faces study the convict standing before them. I turn around and write, "My name is David." Trying to conceal my anxiety, I say, "I am here to help each and every one of you, providing you want it. I couldn't care less if you don't. I'm just as pissed off about being here as I'm sure you are too. In the morning, we'll work on reading, and math in the afternoon. Anybody got any questions before we start?"

"Yeah. You a teacher?"

"No."

"What you in here for?"

"Okay, let's get one thing straight right now before we start. I don't care what you're in here for, but since it seems to be on the mind of every person I meet in here, Let's get it over with. I am here because of weed. You?"

"Coke."

"And you?"

"Heroin."

"And you?"

"Drugs."

"And you?"

"Arson."

"And you?"

"Dope."

"And you?"

"Coke."

"Well, it looks like we all got more in common than we thought," I remark, breathing a nervous sigh of relief.

"We're all dopers," comments a small white kid with acne and freckles that match his fiery hair.

"Speak for yourself, you little burn-out," remarks the arsonist.

"You should talk, Sparky!" hollers a large black inmate from the back of the room.

"Fuck you, motherfuckers!"

"That's ENOUGH!" I interrupt. "Now, let's get started. We are all going to be taking turns at the blackboard. Who wants to go up and write down the vowels? How about you?" I point to the little redheaded troublemaker.

"Fuck off!"

"What's the matter? Didn't you go to school?"

"I got my high school diploma," he brags.

"Where?" I ask.

"Detroit."

"Then why don't you go up there, dude?" asks the black coke dealer from Washington, DC.

"Because I don't know what a *vowel* is. Okay?"

I'm looking at frustrated faces, defeated and abandoned by our education system. These inmates have their high school diplomas and cannot read past the third-grade level! I can't help but feel that when they do get out of here, they'll be recidivists. The heinous crime is being committed by the teachers in the public schools who pass and shove on to somebody else the students, for whatever reason, not to learn and pass the requirements set down. This is not only criminal, but it's also cruel! *Rap, rape; hat, hate; not, note*—we have a long way to go.

"Are seagulls really free? Or are they imprisoned by their appetite to scavenge the local landfill? An easy meal or just something to do? Something to do. Eat, teach. Eat, teach. Eat. Your income is $800 a month. You don't work weekends or any overtime. How much money do you make in one eight-hour day? Anybody?" I point to the black coke dealer from Washington, DC.

"If that was an ounce of cocaine I bought for $800, I'd keep a couple of Gs for myself and sell the rest for $90 each and triple my money."

I return from the Education Department, and glancing around the compound, I see inmates playing games everywhere—basketball (indoor as well as outdoor), tennis, horseshoes, billiards, cards, dominos, ping-pong, and more. The restrictions and limitations from my back condition remind me not to consider. My time is spent in my top bunk reading and rereading Penny's and Sammie's letters and writing them back. My cellmate gives me a book to read by Louis Bromfield, *Paradise Valley*. It's about the romantic lifestyle of being an organic farmer in 1940s Ohio. My soul rests between the pages of this book.

Between the two sets of our bunk beds stands a desk-type table and chair. My bunk has no ladder, so I step on the chair, then onto the top of the desk, then over to my bed. Because of nerve damage to my bladder from my surgeries, I always have to go to the bathroom in the middle of the night. It's my third week here, and while I am sleeping, someone lays a newspaper on top of the desk for my cellmate. That night around 3:00 a.m., climbing out of bed, I step on the newspaper, slip, and crash over backward to the floor. The pain is unbearable. I can't move. Fear of being paralyzed mobilizes me to get up. It hurts to walk, and standing is even worse. I struggle and make it to Medical Services. I get x-rayed and then I am told, "Back to work." The staff will not cooperate, and I remain a tutor until my back gives out altogether. I can no longer stand up. They send for a wheelchair. *Oh, no!* old memories are returning. Medical Services now issues an extra pillow along with a bed board. My cellmate gives up his bottom bunk. I make a sling from a sheet and suspend it from the upper bunk in order to slip my legs up into. Finally, two weeks later, an orthopedic surgeon from St. Luke's, Duluth, is brought in to examine my x-rays. He reveals that two of the wires holding my spine to the large rectangular bracket are broken. He recommends an eight-hour surgery to "pin" another vertebra and remove the broken wires. If I have not already been sitting in a wheelchair, I will have fallen to the floor. The enormity of this news depresses me to the point that my legs already seem paralyzed. Short expressions begin flooding my mind. I feel as if I'm standing in the center of a carousel. The horses are going up and down and round and round. Each horse is carrying its own sign: "No way," "Now what?" "No surgery," "Who cares?" "They don't," "What's next?" "Go home."

The doctor's recommendation leaves me convinced that a second opinion is needed, but what about my rights? Can the government justify shipping me to Springfield, Missouri, chained to a seat on the bus, called diesel therapy, only to have prison surgeons practice a spinal operation on inmate 02188-089? When you're just a faceless number, who cares? Penny—that's who!

After learning the August 17th, 1989, memo from Rod Freitag officially authorizing my medical referral designation to Springfield, she calls her cousin Calvin Andringa. He is like her big brother, and her family is close. Back when Cal was going to college, it was Penny's grandmother (Nana) who paid for his education. Cal couldn't make it to our wedding, but he did call to remind me that if I didn't take good care of Penny, I would have to answer to him even though he was far away in Washington, DC, being an investment banker. His mother, Aunt Bessi (Nana's sister), proudly displays the pictures of the White House wedding of Lyndon Johnson's daughter to Charles Robb. She was there because her son Cal was the best man! It's time to write him a letter.

Dear Cal,

Please know I appreciate your thoughts and prayers. I received another letter today from your mom. She is so special. There will always be a place in my heart for Aunt Bessi. I love her very much. You are truly blessed. The last letter she sent me included stamps, and the prison mailed them back. I guess that's prison life, for they must fear that I will put myself into a box and mail myself home!

I try to keep my spirits up, but I must confess, it gets hard. Especially when I talk to Penny and I hear how the strain is wearing her down. She's a great woman and certainly doesn't deserve all she's getting. I'll never forget the phone call from you when we were about to be married. You said something to the fact that if I didn't take good care of Penny, I'd have you to answer to. Remember?

I have written to the prosecutor for a reconsideration of my sentence, and he said no. So I wrote to the judge (Reynolds), and he said the Rules of Criminal Procedure from 1984 states only the prosecutor can reduce my sentence. As far as sentencing goes, he relies on the US Sentencing Commission Guidelines. What purpose is there for a judge, anyway? With all the power given to the prosecutor and none with the judge, where is our justice? Or should I say, just us!

This whole situation is very bizarre. I'm trying to keep my attitude about it constructive and not become bitter. This afternoon (Tuesday, 3:00 p.m.), Penny had a meeting with Les Aspin's office to discuss what they could do. I have been disabled since June of 1984, by Social Security. I have not worked because of my spinal problems. However, I've been sent by the Bureau of Prisons (BOP) to FPC, Duluth, which is a work camp. I told them when I got here about my situation. My case manager and my counselor both said they didn't want to hear about it. That this is a work camp and I will work. Needless to say, I did what they said, and now my back begins to bother me again. Not to mention, I fell from my top bunk. They took x-rays, and two weeks go by before they bring in a doctor to examine the films. He says he can see the inflammation of the next vertebra down from the three that have been fused. It will need to be pinned to my pelvis. Also, the metal bracket in my spine now has broken wires! He said that it's got to come out before it damages my spinal cord. The whole operation will take eight hours. Just writing about it makes my head spin. With Penny's cancer, finding a home, a job, my prison sentence, and now this! I am close to being overwhelmed. The doctor here told me I have no choice in the matter of where I go and who gets to operate.

I'm sorry, but I do *not* trust the US government. My attorney even so much has said he can't help it that the government lied to me, as he took our money and waved goodbye. So right now, I'm blowing off steam. I don't mean to be burdening you with our problems, Cal, but I feel better just knowing that you care.

I spend my time worrying about Penny, and she spends her time worrying about me. I just wish it could end somehow. I know enough about cancer and Penny's condition to know it's very serious stuff. I've pleaded with the judge for Penny's sake, not mine, and he couldn't care less.

The whole scene is frustrating. If you could drop her a line, I know she would love it.

Thanks for caring!

David

PS: You're the older brother she never had.

* * * * *

Dear Penny:

I have corresponded with David, and in his letter dated August 8, he told me of his latest back problems and the need for another operation.

I have known many people who have had streaks of bad luck and adversity during their lives, but seldom have I heard of an odyssey such as yours and David's. I really do not know where to begin to comment.

Normally, in a situation like this, one could expect you and David to be sincerely asking God, "Why me again?"

However, when the situation becomes this burdensome, I worry you might be asking something more basic, like, "Is there really a God?"

I am sure it is hard for you to believe that this adversity will pass. It must, and it will. I could tell from David's letter that he is close to being overwhelmed, and I worry my letter may find you in the same state of mind.

I can, at a minimum, remind you that you cannot afford to give up. Too many people are counting on both of you. So when the going gets tougher, you just have to be even more determined to see it through.

Please keep my mother informed as to how your treatments are proceeding. I think of you and David often. Obviously, my prayers and most sincere, best wishes are with you.

The most important thing is for you to get better. That will take a lot of positive thinking and taking care of yourself. In time, David will be back. He will have the right to be more than a little bitter and frustrated, but he should come back wiser and more determined to succeed than ever before.

My best to you both. Hang in there, and do not ever give up hope. If you think you can, you will. If you think you won't, you don't.

All my love,
Cal

* * * * *

The Bureau of Prisons (BOP) has two medical facilities. The other being FMC, Rochester, Minnesota. Why am I being sent to Springfield? The Federal Medical Center in Rochester, Minnesota, is 236 miles away, while Springfield is over 800. The inmates begin to tell me the horror stories of Springfield. They talk about the lawless disregard of its many AIDS patients and not to expect coming away without a wheelchair. I hate wheelchairs.

Cal, reassuring Penny, says, "Big brother is watching. There are some very powerful people in Washington interested in the BOP's decision concerning David's case."

A memo from my Inmate Central File states thus:

> Per telephone conversation, please redesignate the abovenamed individual to FMC, Rochester, rather than MCFP, Springfield.

It's now time to transfer. I don't get on the bus, but rather a station wagon with a place in the back for me to lie down.

CHAPTER 3

FMC, Rochester

The ride down to Rochester should be a comfortable ride. However, each bump in the road ripples through my body as pain coming and pain going. The "hack" (guard) driving the car takes on an extremely hostile attitude. I get the feeling it's directed more toward me than the car.

Entering into Rochester, the home of the famous Mayo Clinic, I notice just how clean the city is. There is no unconfined trash typically associated with curbs and gutters, and the sidewalks look free of cigarette butts. This city is internationally recognized for the Mayo Clinic, and it prides itself before many foreign and domestic dignitaries, even the president of the United States!

I'm not getting the reception of a dignitary, I can tell by the expressions of the people looking at me, in the government car with its uniformed driver while they stand at the stoplight. I am one of "them" heading toward the other side of town where society's unfortunate are sent to be punished.

As we make our way, a series of large brick buildings, all the same color, come into view. They are all surrounded by a pair of high chain-link fences. Rolls and rolls of razor wire fastened at the top shine bright in the midday sun. as I walk with the guard toward the prison, the impression of concentrated sadness begins to overcome me. When I arrived at PPC, Duluth, I was still in shock and numbed by my fading denial. Remember, Duluth doesn't have fences. It merely looks like a busy Army camp. Now I'm seeing a federal prison for the first time. Me, a patron, a prisoner, but certainly no criminal.

What will they do to me? Is surgery really necessary? Do I trust these people? Will I get along? How tough are these convicts?

The Bureau of Prisons classifies all its prisoners according to their criminal history. They have six custody-level rankings. I am a level 1. Don't forget, I'm coming from a camp that I've voluntarily surrendered to. FMC, Rochester, harbors security levels 1–5! Level 6 inmates are caged in the maximum security prison in Marion, Illinois.

After receiving, intake screening, and orientation, I find myself assigned to the medical-surgical unit, building 10-1. I enter my two-man cell. It's a room on the first floor with an overpowering view of the disgusting razor-wire wall. It is a formidable sight. A constant reminder that I am not going anywhere!

As I lie on my bed and stare out the window, the razor wire reflects the night-lights in the yard. To leave this place, I close my eyes. Thoughts of Penny are my only disguise. My heart's with the wind, my spirit flying. My body behind, asleep, there lying. *Oh, Penny, can you feel my hand upon your head? I am here tonight beside your bed!*

"COUNT TIME!" the guard yells as he patrols the hall, looking in each room. When he looks in mine, he sees a narrow room with a bed, desk, and locker on the left and a desk, locker, and bed on the right. I'm lying on my hospital-type bed with its electric water mattress and extra pillow on the right by the window. Across from my bed and next to my desk in the corner is a sink. I'm told it was installed for an elderly orthodox Jewish rabbi from New York who was convicted for crimes having to do with diamonds.

I've never had a lady doctor before. After a series of examinations, she concludes that I remain on no-duty status (medically unassigned), with no prolonged standing, stooping, sitting, or bending, and one-hour bed rest two times a day. She then orders physical rehabilitation, and a brace for my right foot, which is experiencing the "drop-foot syndrome." I also receive a cane to ambulate. I sign a release so she can acquire my medical records from Madison. In the meantime, I enter classes in deep muscle relaxation and self-image, taught by Dr. Imp, head of the psychology department.

The first inmate I get to know is Garry McClain, a polite, soft-spoken forty-one-year-old from the bluegrass state of Kentucky. His short graying hair and well-trimmed silver beard leave him looking like a Kenny Rogers double. His sense of humor combined with his Southern charm have had a lot to do with him being married six times to five women.

Garry is a Vietnam veteran with very severe medical problems and a long history of extensive medical care. He has suffered from three heart attacks—at one of the attacks, he was actually pronounced dead—and thirteen arrhythmic attacks. After suffering from his second arrhythmic attack, he volunteered to be a test case for the new, untested implantable defibrillator, at that time unapproved by the FDA, along with an untested, experimental antiarrhythmic drug (amiodarone). In response to this treatment, while being filmed for a television news spot. I said, "If it will help others, I'll, do it." The implant failed. He had to be rushed by helicopter to University of Louisville for emergency removal as it would not stop "shocking" his heart with its seven-hundred-volt jolts.

Garry's judgment became blind with the overwhelming threat of premature death, and having a young family he dearly wanted to provide a home for left him extremely vulnerable to the persistent suggestions from a government informant with the promise of making some "easy money" from one cocaine deal.

Garry has now had the defibrillator replaced again with a "newer model," and he is presently, according to the Mayo Clinic, the longest-surviving patient in the United States.

When Garry learns of my legal situation, he directs me to the law library and introduces me to another pair of inmates, a lawyer from St. Paul and a judge from Chicago. The judge, hearing that I am a guideline case, retrieves the 1988 Revised Edition Federal Sentencing Guideline Manual and hands it to me.

"So this is that big complicated book my lawyer referred to. He believed that this was going to be declared unconstitutional," I remark.

FEDERAL SENTENCING GUIDELINES MANUAL

1988 REVISED EDITION

UNITED STATES SENTENCING
COMMISSION

Effective November 1, 1987

Including
Amendments to Guidelines and Official Commentary
(Effective January 15 and June 15, 1988)
Supplementary Illustrations
Sentencing Act of 1987
Criminal Fine Improvements Act of 1987
Model Sentencing Forms

The publisher will provide updated revisions of the Federal Sentencing Guidelines, Official Commentaries, and other related materials as issued.

ST. PAUL, MINN.
WEST PUBLISHING CO.
1988

"It's the law of the land," says the judge. "Read pages 62 and 63, the 'Drug Quantity Table,'" recommends Jim, the lawyer from St. Paul. Reading page 62 for the first time, I'm beginning to tremble. The book becomes heavy. I open it up to the pages and read about level 26. This is the level the government has put me at. In order to be a level 26, according to the guidelines, I had to have had 1,000 to 3,999 marijuana plants. Holy crap! I had 162. I read on. Level 16 is 100 to 199 marijuana plants. Raising my voice and becoming visibly upset, I blurt out, "What's so complicated about this book? Got too many pages? It's written in English, for crying out loud! How can this be?" I ask, bewildered, shocked, and angry.

Jim stops his typewriter and, with a calm, confident voice of an attorney, says, "You got a bad lawyer."

The judge advises, "You got a good case, son. I suggest you file a petition against your lawyer for ineffective assistance of counsel."

I wonder, Why did my attorney, Gerald P. Boyle, advise me to plead guilty to the conspiracy in the indictment and stipulate to 340 pounds as the weight that was to be the basis of my sentence? He did not tell me that the definition of *marijuana*, as given within the federal code, excluded stalks of marijuana, nor did he tell me that case law from the federal courts also specifically excluded stalks, stems, and dirt from the weight of the marijuana that was to be used as the basis for sentencing.

It's October now, and I'm on a crash course in learning how to put together a pro se habeas corpus 2255 appeal. I'm sure glad I took typing in high school. If you want to find me, I am at the typewriter in the law library.

I can't wait to phone Penny and tell her the news. I have to be careful what I say, though, for our calls are being monitored. I even have to watch what I write because our letters are read by the staff before they're sealed and mailed off.

I have got to stay out of trouble. I don't want to participate in any mischief. My inmate neighbor is making shampoo booze. He gets ahold of uncooked bread dough smuggled past the guard in the kitchen and uses it for yeast. He then empties out a shampoo bottle, puts in the dough, sugar, and fruit juice, screws the cap back on, flips the top spout up, removes the dryer exhaust hose, places it inside, replaces the hose to the vent, turns on the dryer, and proceeds to "cook" his concoction into shampoo booze.

It's mail call, and I get a letter from Samantha.

Dear Dad,

Sorry I haven't wrote you in a long time. I just feel bad all the time. Mom always gets mad at me because I can't get up for school. All I want to do is sleep. It was good to talk to you. You sounded real good, and that made Mom happy. If you got my last letter, that's all straightened out now. I still want you home and Mom still has changed but refuses to admit it, but it's all worked out. I'm still living with Mom. So I'm really sorry if I upset you. I never should have wrote that, but I was real upset, and I still am, but Mom ain't gonna change, so I'm trying to live with her. She ain't too bad, really, except when she's in a bad mood, then watch out! But we seem to be getting along so far. I can't wait till we are a family again. It will be so much fun. I miss you a lot.

Well, I better go. I love you very much and miss you a lot.

Love,
Samantha

PS: I sure wouldn't mind being fourteen.

Penny and Sam are moving in with Bea and Obie, her mom and dad. They will be living upstairs, above Obie's Cobblestone Bar and Restaurant. I make my collect call to Obie, and he says, "David, not to worry. I'll take care of the girls." I love that man. I don't know what we will do without him.

I get a visit from Penny and Sam today. My little girl is growing up without me. I want to warn any boy who makes her cry that he will have to deal with me. Samantha's shed enough tears. Her teacher has the class take out a sheet of paper and write a one-page essay about their father. He turns to Samantha and says, "Sam, you'll probably have trouble coming up with a page." Why are people so cruel? I will have a talk with him when I get out. When will that be? How long will it take?

I become obsessed with learning the legal system from my new-found friends at the law library. They teach me how the law library works. How to cross-reference (Shepardize) case law. I learn how to apply the law to the facts of a case. How to interpret a judge's dissenting opinion to better understand a case. I'm becoming a jailhouse lawyer fast. It must run in the family; after all, my dad's father was a lawyer. His name was Hiram Price, and everyone knew him as Hi. I can't imagine hanging out a lawyer's shingle that says, "Hi Price, Attorney at Law."

My grandfather spent a lifetime in community service. He was an early organizer of the Pure Milk Association. First president of the Elkhorn Pure Milk Local, an office he held for twenty-three years. He was also the director of the third PMA district for several terms. He was past member of the Walworth County Board, was a long-time member of the Potters School Board, and was chairman of the Steering Committee that organized the Elkhorn Common School District in 1956. He was elected the first clerk of this district, which he held until he resigned after the death of his wife, Martha, in 1961. In 1965, when Grandpa was eighty-four years old and I was just in high school, I remember asking him, "Why did you quit being a lawyer and go farming when you had to farm with horses?" Hiram was a big man with a full head of gray hair. There was still power in his handshake and wisdom in his words. He got up from his kitchen table, his chew hitting the spittoon, and, like he was preaching a sermon, said, "Because it was more noble to walk behind the farts of a horse than it was to be an attorney!"

You would have liked my grandpa—everyone did—and you will like my dad. Everybody does. I can't tell you what it must feel like to bury your eldest child then lose your second to prison, but I can tell you, it's been hard on Mom and Dad. Now, I learn I could be losing Penny. She is back in the hospital with pain in her chest and abdomen. Immediately I entertain thoughts of escaping, but like a caged lion, I can only roar. I'm still haunted by the words "Lots of inmates have relatives that die while they're in prison." In the meantime, I begin to put together a motion for release pending review. The inmates in the law library all tell me to concentrate on my habeas corpus 2255 instead. I follow their advice and work even harder.

Meanwhile, my friend Garry writes to a nonprofit organization called ECHO (Educational Concerns for Hydrogen and Oxygen) from Delano, Minnesota. They donate several books to the prison library. The two most popular are *The Peroxide Story*, by George Borewell, and *Oxygen Therapies*, by Ed McCabe. I learn that the medical industry is supported by the large pharmaceutical industry, which trains and controls the doctors as well. Their big money is made *not* in health and happiness but in sickness and misery. There is no incentive in preventing and curing disease. So we are all deceived into believing that in order to get well from having cancer, it's surgery, radiation, and chemotherapy (cut, burn, and poison). They have gone overboard promoting their drugs to the public, even the ones with many known side effects.

The inmates don't trust the establishment and are more than willing to try alternative treatments. However, it must be done on the sly. No one in authority must know. I begin to circulate the books around the med-surgical 10-1 unit when I meet Frank Schwiesch, a new arrival from MCC, Chicago. The dark circles around his eyes, along with his fifty-six-year-old pale-gray complexion from being in solitary confinement too long, leave Frank looking like he has come here to die. Frank got rough treatment in Chicago by the hacks because of what he told the judge at his sentencing hearing, more than his ties to the Mob. At his sentencing, the lady judge asked Frank if he had anything to say for himself before she passed sentence. Frank replied, "Your pussy stinks! I can smell it from here."

"Forty years! Get him out of my courtroom!" she said as she slammed the gavel down.

Frank has continually been beaten until he now urinates blood. When I hear this, I ask, "Is that why you're here?"

Sadly, he remarks, "No. They say I have a tumor under my tongue and they want to cut off my lower jaw." I ask about the burn marks on his arms. Frank answers, "I got skin cancer. That's where they burned it off."

My next question is, "What did the doctors tell you?"

"Fuck 'em. I can't stand doctors."

"Oh?"

"I've been shot twice and I didn't need no doctor."

"Really? Where were you shot?"

Frank shows me the back of his left knee. The scar is wide. The bullet also leaves him without a calf muscle. Then he lifts his T-shirt, and there, sticking out from just under the skin in the middle of his back, is the flatted remains of a bullet!

I introduce Frank to the Peroxide books. Later, he wants to try drinking the mixture. He understands about the need for secrecy, so he gets permission from his doctor to have a plastic gallon jug in his room for drinking water. When enough water is gone from the gallon, it's replaced with hydrogen peroxide. That is still a little too strong of a concentration; however, Tommy Zito has just gone to the "hole" for having an unauthorized bottle. In order to have a bottle of peroxide, you must have a doctor's prescription. Tommy will not tell where he acquired his bottle (me). We miss Tommy for thirty days.

Frank begins drinking his peroxide water three times a day on an empty stomach and spends the week in bed. Fever ravages his body while his bed linen is soaked with sweat. I bring Frank his new bottle of peroxide. I get bottles of peroxide prescribed to me by my lady doctor. All told, she keeps me supplied with peroxide by writing thirty-three prescriptions with multiple refills.

I explain to Frank the detoxifying process. That it's just all the bad cancer cells leaving his body. Two more weeks and two more bottles of peroxide, and his skin cancer sore starts changing. Frank is getting excited, and now he wants to drink even more. I explain that more isn't better. That he must continue his diluted (five-ounce water to one-ounce peroxide) mixture three times a day on an empty stomach and have patience.

Nearly two months pass. Frank is no longer bedridden. His skin color is back. He is spending time outside in the yard. One day, the guards come and take him to the Mayo Clinic. It's time for his scheduled surgery to remove his jaw. Later that same day, Frank is standing in my room, unable to conceal his joy.

I ask, "What happened?"

He replies, "They canceled my surgery. The doctor seems to think they must have gotten it all on the biopsy!"

"What did they say about your skin cancer?" I inquire.

Holding out his arm, he says, "Look. It's gone too!"

I can't tell you how happy I am for Frank.

Jim Layton, a large lumberjack from Oregon, is sent here to have heart bypass surgery. He cannot walk up one flight of stairs without running out of air. Jim is the owner of a logging company. One of his cutters cut down the wrong tree. The tree was at the edge and on the bend of a popular road. It was also a tree marked for the endangered spotted owl. Jim is in prison for eighteen months because of a "politically correct" prosecution.

I get Jim his bottle of peroxide, and within weeks, he is walking the track around the yard. It takes Jim a week to drink down a bottle of peroxide. He continues the program and finds himself getting stronger with more energy. The Mayo Clinic does more tests on Jim and ultimately cancels his bypass surgery.

Dick Cardall is a seventy-six-year-old lawyer from Utah. He originally was diagnosed with prostrate cancer. It has now spread up his spine. I meet Dick at the Rehab Department, in the bottom of building 9. Building 9 is where the seriously ill inmates live. He has heard of what has been happening in building 10-1 with inmates drinking peroxide. I get Dick the books and a bottle of peroxide. He, too, eventually soaks his bed linen from a high fever. After the fever breaks, he discovers his pain is now manageable. I meet up with Dick in rehab. He gets off the bicycle he is peddling, gets down on all fours (hands and knees), and curls up his spine like a cat. "I could never do this before," he says. "I know I'm going to die. My cancer is too far along in my bones, and believe me, bone cancer hurts. The peroxide has taken that pain almost away, and I'm grateful for that. God bless you, David."

That is the last time I see Dick. He is gone.

Joe Aiuypa is an eighty-four-year-old man who has just received a twenty-year sentence. I'm told he was the head boss of the Mafia in Chicago during the 1970s. He lives in the next cell down from me. He has many other Mafia inmates always around him, looking after him, bringing him extra fruit, etc. Herbie Blitzstein cuts his garlic every day. Joe is referred to as the old man. He has been bedridden with gout. Yes, peroxide makes its way into the old man. Soon, he is seen pushing his wheelchair around the track several times a day.

One day he walks past my cell on his way to the visitors' room. His clothes clean and pressed and his thinning hair all in place, he looks perfect.

I say as he walks by, "Have a nice visit, Joe."

Within minutes, he is back. I ask, "No visitor, Joe?"

He barks, "If you wanna call a lawyer and an FBI agent a visitor."

"What did you tell them?"

"I told them to go fuck themselves," he says as he proudly and defiantly walks back to his cell.

I want to help everyone.

Dominick has advanced liver cancer. It leaves him in much pain and yellow with jaundice. I mention to Vinnie, "I feel sorry for Dominick. I hear the government won't allow him visitors, not even his son from back home in New York."

Vinnie says, "Don't you feel sorry for Dominick. I know him. He's a coldblooded killer. He would drive around New York City pretending to be lost, and when he could lure a black kid to his car for directions, he'd shoot 'em dead." Vinnie goes on to say, "I was with him once when he did this, and when I asked him, 'What the hell did ya do that for?' Dominick's answer was, 'That's one less nigger to worry about.'"

I don't feel sorry for Dominick.

We have a new arrival from Leavenworth. He is a sixty-one-year-old aerospace engineer from Los Angeles, California. He is a small slightly balding man with wire-rimmed glasses and is an intelligent conversationalist. Fred fits right in at the library but looks way out of place in this prison. He can't be a criminal. Obviously an educated man, he is the kind of person I have no trouble getting to know and like. We soon become friends. I learn his wife, Kirstin, is from Copenhagen, Denmark. Penny's mother, Bea, is from Copenhagen too. Bea's older sister, Aunt Sonja, lives in Copenhagen only blocks away from Kirstin's mother. What a small world!

Fred is also fighting for justice, both legal and medical. His legal papers read like a Hollywood movie script. Fred and his codefendant, Sammy Daily, had a little real estate development company.

They used borrowed funds from Indian Springs State Bank of Kansas City. The bank failed. The Justice Department filed a thirty-two-count indictment against Fred and Sammy. A six-month trial found them not guilty of all thirty-two counts. However, the government superseded the indictment information with a charge of conspiracy, and according to the jury foreman, "You must be guilty of something, or the government wouldn't have gone to so much trouble." Found guilty of conspiracy to commit wire fraud, Fred finds himself in Leavenworth, serving four years.

There in Leavenworth, Fred meets an inmate named Heinrich "Harry" Rupp. Harry tells Fred the real story behind the company that was the one responsible for the failing of the Kansas City Bank, Global International Airways.

This company was a CIA front for covert activities, and he (Harry) was a pilot for them for many years. Harry had been a contract agent for the CIA since after World War II. He had flown many covert activities, including flying guns to the Contras over the objection of the US Congress (the Boland Amendment). The Contras paid for these illegally shipped guns, not with a credit card, but with drugs. The logic of having drug money pay for the pressing needs of the Contras appealed to a number of people who became involved in the covert war. Indeed, senior US policy makers were not immune to the idea that drug money was a perfect solution to the Contra's funding problems, according to the Senate Foreign Relations Subcommittee on Narcotics, Terrorism, and International Operations 1,196-page published report titled "Drugs, Law Enforcement, and US Foreign Policy."

Harry continues to tell Fred that it was he who flew George Bush, William Casey, and others to Paris, France, in October 1980, where they used their CIA connections to secure a deal with Iran to continue holding the fifty-two American hostages in order to help defeat Jimmy Carter in the 1980 election. In return, they (Reagan-Bush team) promised billions of dollars in military hardware to the Ayatollah Khomeini. George Bush was an ex–CIA director fired by Jimmy Carter. No private citizen shall interfere with the foreign policy of the United States government, and to do so is a violation of the Logan Act, a very serious crime bordering on treason. Was it a coincidence that on Inauguration Day, the very instant Ronald Reagan was sworn into office, the fifty-two hostages were released?

100th Congress — 1st Session • January 6–December 22, 1987

JOHN F. KENNEDY
Memorial Library
CAL STATE L A.

Senate Report 17 890

Depository Item

No. 216

IRAN-CONTRA INVESTIGATION
APPENDIX A, VOLUME 1
SOURCE DOCUMENTS

United States Congressional Serial Set

Serial Number 13740

United States Government Printing Office
Washington : 1989

60

DRUGS, LAW ENFORCEMENT AND FOREIGN POLICY

A REPORT

PREPARED BY THE

SUBCOMMITTEE ON
TERRORISM, NARCOTICS AND INTERNATIONAL
OPERATIONS

OF THE

COMMITTEE ON FOREIGN RELATIONS
UNITED STATES SENATE

DECEMBER 1988

Printed for the use of the Committee on Foreign Relations

U.S. GOVERNMENT PRINTING OFFICE

96-945

WASHINGTON : 1989

$p \cdot 6 \cdot 1$

For sale by the Superintendent of Documents, U.S. Government Printing Office
Washington, DC 20402

Harry goes on to explain that the CIA had a man on the Kansas Bank's board of directors, an Iranian-born, naturalized American named Farhad Azima, who also owned Global International Airways. Global was the one responsible for failing the bank, by defaulting on its $15 million loan, not Fred.

Fred learns later that this information was not brought before the grand jury. He also learns that the assistant US attorney (Lloyd Monroe) of the Justice Department was told by higher-up government officials in the CIA to back off Global and look for a more politically correct prosecution in the name of national security.

In the meantime, I help Fred with his pro se motion for bail pending appeal.

Fred believes the government gave him cancer when he first came to prison. Once there, he developed a lump in his groin, and for the next several months, the physician's assistant (PA) would not allow him to see the doctor. When Fred finally does get to see the doctor, they ship him here to FMC, Rochester. The Mayo Clinic diagnoses Fred with cancer of the groin and removes his penis. Further tests show his cancer has spread into his pelvic lymph nodes, like Penny.

Fred now drinks hydrogen peroxide, too. He dilutes his solution with orange juice and goes through the detoxification process like the others. We become very busy working in the law library on our motions to get out of here. He learns from his case manager that *60 Minutes* wants to interview him. Fred is so excited. Then he learns Everett Lemester, a member of the bank's board of directors, who is coming forward to testify to the truth, has blown up in his car. The blast is so huge the only identification comes from his personalized golf clubs that are in his back seat. The death is an unsolved homicide. The *60 Minute* interview is canceled.

It's December now, and I am ready to file my pro se habeas corpus 2255 petition. On December 10, 1989, Penny files an affidavit in support of my petition, and on this very same day, Jeffrey Dahmer writes a letter to his judge:

Dear Judge Gardner,

My name is Jeff Dahmer. On September 20, 1988, I was arrested in Milwaukee, Wisconsin, for taking pictures of a thirteen-year-old minor. On September 27, 1988, I was released on bail from the Milwaukee County Jail. On May 23, 1989, after having entered a plea of guilty in your court, I received my sentence. It was as follows: one year on work release at CCC and five years of probation. I have, as of this date, served six months and four days of my sentence. Sir, I have always believed that a man should be willing to assume responsibility for the mistakes that he makes in life. That is why I entered a plea of guilty to the crime of which I was charged. During my stay at CCC, I have had a chance to look at my life from an angle that was never presented to me before. What I did was deplorable. The world has enough misery in it without my adding more to it. Sir, I can assure you that it will never happen again. This is why, Judge Gardner, I am requesting from you a sentence modification so that I may be allowed to continue my life as a productive member of our society.

Respectfully yours,
Jeff Dahmer

Mr. Steinle, feel free to alter and correct this letter in any manner you see fit.

CHAPTER 4

The 2255

Happy New Year 1990! I feel confident as I address my page motion under 28 USC Section 2255 to vacate, set aside, or correct sentence by a person in federal custody, along with a thirteen-page memorandum in support of section 2255 motion, to the Eastern District of Wisconsin.

* * * * *

Ground 1: Denial of the right to the effective assistance of counsel.

Supporting Facts: Defendant tendered a guilty plea that was a product of his lawyer's unprofessional conduct and lack of his attempting to represent defendant at a competent level. Gerald Boyle did not do any research and gave advice to defendant that was incompetent. He told defendant that he knew little, if anything, about the new sentencing laws and assumed that they would be held unconstitutional by the Supreme Court, therefore, made no effort to present the issue of their proper application. He told defendant to plead guilty or else face a minimum mandatory of five years, which was grossly erroneous, though defendant did not know and accepted this as true. His assistant agreed with the prosecutor on the weight (dried) of the marijuana plants of 340 pounds at the arraignment on September 23, 1988, and did not even appear there. And the actual weight was not relevant to the guidelines. Attorney Boyle was completely disconcerned with all the legal aspects of the case, because he wasn't getting paid the additional fee requested and then demanded. He told defendant that he was getting "burned by you" and demanded his $9,000 right outside the courtroom before the guilty plea was entered. His assistant told defendant to not contest the erroneously agreed-upon dry weight of the marijuana because it would cost at least $2,000 to have experts discredit the poundage. All the lawyer could discuss right up to the time defendant was sentenced was what the defendant had owed to him—i.e., "I wish I had never taken you as a client. You're a losing proposition." And he only read the presentence report two days before the court-imposed sentence. Attorney Boyle was merely "hoping" the court would take into consideration the stalks and stems, which were irrelevant to computing and applying the guidelines. Further, his erroneous "theory" at sentencing was to get defendant "sentenced outside the guidelines. "You deserve a break." He also told defendant that he had a "good" judge. "The judge and I go way back. I'm going to do you a lot of good." Of course, attorney Boyle made no effort to see the guidelines correctly applied at sentencing.

Ground 2: The US Sentencing Commission Guidelines were incorrectly applied resulting in an illegal sentence.

Supporting Facts: The defendant was indicted and pled guilty to count one of the indictment. The court imposed a mandatory sentence of fifty-one months, the minimum required, relying on the US Sentencing Commission Guidelines requiring a sentence under level 26 of section 2Dl.l(a)(3). At the sentencing, defendant objected to the court's reliance on the government's calculation of the weight of the marijuana. Defendant disagreed as to the portion that could be called a usable product and hence considered in the total weight. In addition, the presentence report stated that there were 162 marijuana plants involved. On page 1 in the addendum, the government entered no objection to the contents of the presentence report. For a level 26, the number of plants must be between 1,000 and 3,999 This level guideline was used as a result of an improper conversion of the weight of the (340 pounds total) marijuana plants (stalks and all) into its equivalent kilograms of usable marijuana. That calculation was improper and incorrect. The proper application of the guidelines is to count the number of plants involved (162), which requires a level sixteen (16) sentence (100–199 plants). In addition, the guidelines require a two-point deduction for the defendant's "acceptance of his responsibility," hence resulting in a level 14 sentence (fifteen to twenty-one months) of incarceration. In summary, the court incorrectly applied the guidelines to the weight of the marijuana plants (340 estimated pounds) when it was the number of plants that the guidelines should have applied (162, see p. 7, paragraph 5 presentence report).

Ground 3: Denial of the right to appeal by defendant's lack of funds to retain counsel and his ignorance and misleading statements by counsel of record.

Supporting Facts: The attorney who had been representing defendant wanted his nine thousand dollars ($9,000) so much and refused to do anything else for defendant except mislead defendant after sentencing. Defendant could not afford to hire counsel by reason of poverty for an appeal to the Seventh Circuit Court of Appeals. Counsel had told defendant that he would be with defendant till he was released and advised him only to write a letter asking the court to reconsider his sentence. Counsel had a "theory" and, of course, was not stated but only to mislead defendant before and after sentence because he was nine thousand dollars short of the increased retainer after agreeing to take the case for $5,000, which defendant paid. Further, defendant is not trained at law, has a limited education, and could not, nor did not, know how to file any appeal and was without counsel, nor did he know how to obtain representation without paying a fee to an attorney. Counsel just plainly refused to file an appeal because it was his wrongful or unprofessional treatment of the case that would have been the basis of the appeal and he did not desire to raise his own. He demanded the defendant sign an illegal agreement to garnish the possible workmen's compensation benefits just prior to sentencing. All he was concerned with was getting the money, and without it, defendant was getting no effective assistance of counsel. Defendant, therefore, was denied his right to appeal the conviction and sentence.

Ground 4: The plea was coerced under the facts alleged in ground 1 (ineffective assistance of counsel), and neither the court, under rule 11 of the Federal Rules of Criminal Procedure, nor his lawyer informed petitioner of the essential elements and the defendant's defenses.

Supporting Facts: Neither the court, nor the attorney, when accepting the plea, informed petitioner of the elements of the alleged charges, knowledge, and intent. This denied petitioner the right to the defense of mistake, which he stated on the record to this effect, when the court took the plea. Further, the court did not establish a factual basis for accepting the plea. This violated rule 11 and, upon denial of effective counsel, made the plea involuntary and unintelligent.

Argument

Petitioner pled guilty without an understanding of the law as to the relative facts and without being advised by counsel of any of his defenses. Counsel's performance was so inadequate that it might be considered that petitioner was represented by no more than a warm body. Counsel did not know what the guidelines were and how they were to be applied. Counsel, however, did not consider such requirements and demands of a competent lawyer. He had his mind on the additional amount owed to him by petitioner. These are fundamental defects in the proceedings that constitute a miscarriage of justice and warrant the court granting the relief.

Petitioner's sentence is in excess of the United States Sentencing Commission Guidelines that resulted by the court relying on the weight of the marijuana, not the amount of plants involved. Petitioner's offense level is drastically changed in light of the correct and proper application, and mindful of the facts that warrant the court to grant an evidentiary hearing on the issue of the excessive sentence, the court should grant petitioner a prompt remedy. Counsel's total misconduct and into the record appears his false hopes, some of which he called a miracle, shows that he did not really believe or even know what would happen and the lawyer had a duty to inform petitioner of the application of the guidelines in their proper perspective and correct application. But counsel merely hoped the court would impose a sentence outside and under the guidelines, which was the hope he instilled into a person that owed him a lot of money and could not pay. Petitioner paid, but paid with the ineffective assistance of counsel. In the interest of justice, the court should conduct a thorough inquiry.

Conclusion

The court should hold an evidentiary hearing and, upon finding of the facts, grant the relief sought. The second day of January 1990.

David L. Price
Pro se petitioner
Reg. No. 02188-089
Post Office Box 4600
Rochester, MN 55903

* * * * *

I mail it out to my good friend, neighbor, and also Social Security representative, Odel Gigante, to make copies in his office and file them with the court. I go back to my cell and write to Penny.

Dear Penny,

I sure miss you! Yesterday when I was at the library, I read how long 2255s usually take for the court to finalize them. It was depressing. However, I am still holding on to my faith that God will bring me back to you soon. The guy that helped me with mine will be going home, maybe next week. So I should be excited that they do work. Right now I am working to prepare my reply to the response from R. Jeffery Wagner. I feel confident, so you need not worry, dear. I hope Wagner doesn't do like most prosecutors and try to lead the judge with out-of-context quotes and irrelevant case law. Believe me, Penny, they will do it. I met an attorney who is in here because his client lied to him. Anyhow, he was telling me that the law profession as a whole is entirely a respectable bunch. He claims that it is the few bad criminal lawyers who ruin it for the rest. To be a corporate lawyer, international lawyer, estate lawyer, etc. is very hard, and the integrity is impeccable! However, if you can't hack it, you can always be a criminal lawyer. They are the ones who had a tough time getting through law school. Their clients are criminals instead of top-notch, law-abiding businessmen. And another point he brought out was paying an attorney for a guilty plea. Whatever money he cons you into paying, anything he has to do on your behalf comes out of his pocket and, hence, makes the net profit come down. So in reality, his incentive is to do as little as possible for you. He said most lawyers don't have a whole lot of respect for the criminal lawyers. Boy, I sure can see why, hey?

I am struggling with my diet and exercise. One thing I don't want to become is lazy. I'm sure that will not happen. I have a lot of mail to get caught up on, and then I will feel better about it. I must write our Baha'i friend Bob Amerson. I once asked Bob, "If you could only have three words on your gravestone, what would they be?" He said he wants his to say, "He Recognized Baha'u'llah." Right now, mine feels like it should read, "He Went Home!" You know, Penny, how important our spirituality is. We must never neglect our spiritual growth, learning and applying the Baha'i principles of life.

I love you, Penny. Somehow, just knowing that makes all these trials and tribulations seem less important.

Good night for now.

Love,
David

I love mail call. Penny always has a letter there for me. Even the guards enjoy her colorful, creative envelopes. Nobody gets, more mail than I do, except perhaps Jimmy Bakker. The inmates all share in my anxiety of expecting news from the court. The suspense can even be felt as the days begin to become weeks. The waiting is driving me nuts! I now begin to hear the stories of the vindictive prosecutor, so I keep busy researching case law, and to my delight, I find a case prosecuted at the same time (1988) with the same number of marijuana plants (100–199) from the same circuit (seventh), only with a different result.

I put together a powerful four-page supplemental memorandum in support of my 2255 motion and file it on my little girl's birthday (January 21). I feel like I've just launched a rocket and I'm eagerly waiting to hear the impact.

My motion hits the Milwaukee Federal Courthouse with a splash. Two days after my supplemental memorandum is filed, my judge (Reynolds) reads it and recuses himself. The clerk of courts assigns me a new judge, the Honorable Thomas J. Curran. He reads my pleadings, and when his January 26 order arrives in the prison mail, I grab the envelope from the guard, tear it open, and read aloud, "The court has reviewed the motion of David L. Price. Judge Reynolds has recused himself, and the case has been randomly reassigned to this court. The court has reviewed the motion and finds that Mr. Price has arguably stated grounds for relief due to ineffective assistance of counsel." Holding back the applause, I continue, "The United States attorney is ordered to file an answer or other pleading within twenty days of the date of this Order." A small celebration erupts. It feels like the playoffs. High fives are everywhere. Hope gets to fan the flames of freedom today.

My dear Samantha,

I am so sorry I missed your birthday. I want to remind you how happy I have been over the years being your father. I remember the day you were born, and my life was never the same again. How we weathered the good times and the hard times. It's not easy being a young person, and it's not easy being a parent. I think the two of us did pretty well.

I remember your hug on Father's Day, the call that came when I was in the hospital, the many Christmas presents over the years, your smile when you helped me build our treehouse, and how proud I am of you.

You are my special friend, and I thank you.

Lots of love,
Dad

PS: After you read this, would you please go give Mom one of your hugs and tell her it's from me?

It's mail call again.

Hi, Dave,

Did I tell you I have your Valentine's Day card sitting on my desk? The great big one about "kissing." It's true, you know, about kissing and the location. You know where, all right. It's like I say, the first two days we are staying at a hotel. Just you and me alone! Maybe even more than two days!

I counted your last letter to me, and it was number 73. I never thought I would ever get seventy-three letters from my husband. Funny how things happen, only our situation has never been funny. But the good news is, we both got a lot of practice in writing. I am just glad you enjoy my mail. I have always tried to make you as happy as I can. Thanks for appreciating me. It's nice to hear.

Dell was in last night. He and Sharon were in for their Friday-night fish. I was sitting at the table with them when Samantha came up to me and said Cal was on the phone upstairs. So I quickly ran upstairs and talked to him. He wanted to make sure he hasn't missed anything. He made me go over the situation so he could take notes. I told him again about Judge Reynolds recusing himself and your letter from the clerk of courts stating your case was reassigned to Judge Curran, stating he reviewed the 2255 motion and finds that you have arguably stated grounds for relief due to ineffective assistance of counsel. Cal thinks what will happen next is that Wagner will ask for an extension to review the motion, and he will probably oppose it, saying it has no merit. That is what Cal thinks, but the good news is, he is on top of it and he has hired heavy hitters to get you out. Cal says Wagner has my case messed up and he is goddamn sick of all the mistakes that were made. You never should have gone to prison. Cal says, "Not to worry, big brother in Washington is watching." We are making signif- icant progress, and he keeps telling me you *will* ultimately succeed!

David, I want confidence and good feelings about our future. I am working on strengthening my faith. I hope it is okay that I lean on your shoulders.

With all kinds of love,
your wife,
Penny

It's February 16, 1990, and I gather my legal notes and sit down to write Calvin Andringa, president of the Ashton Group, 1025 Thomas Jefferson Street, Washington, DC.

Dear Cal:

First, let me thank you for taking an interest in my situation. God only knows how I will ever be able to repay you. In our recent phone conversa- tion, you mentioned the issue of *law* regarding my sentencing. Both the statute and the Federal Sentencing Guidelines support my case. Also, I am including three (3) separate cases that addressed the issue of plants correctly, one of which happens to be in the same circuit (seventh) and dealing with the *same* number of marijuana plants.

The statute applicable to my case is the 1988 version along with the 1988 Federal Guidelines and the appropriate case examples listed below.

Federal Sentencing Guideline
Manual 1988 Edition

2D1.1(a)(3) The base level is specified in the drug quantity table.

Schedule I. Marijuana

1 marijuana/cannabis plant = 100 grams of marijuana (10 plants = 1 kilogram).

Support for the interpretation of the guidelines that the number of plants is the proper measure when measuring live plants as found in 21 USC Section 841 (b) (1)(D), which provides the penalty in certain cases under section 841 (a)(l)t. "In the case of less than fifty kilograms of marijuana, except in the case of one hundred or more marijuana plants regardless of weight...such person shall...be sentenced to a term of imprisonment of not more than five years."

My next example comes from the same circuit as mine (seventh) and also coincidently concerning the same number of marijuana plants. *US v. Weidner*, 703 F. Supp. 1350 1352 (ND IND, September 1988). Sentencing Memorandum, Miller, Jr., Robert L., District Judge.

a. The Quantity of Marijuana

"Section 2D1.1(a)(3) directs the court to refer to the drug quantity table to determine the base offense level. That table provides that the base offense level for an offense involving at least 100, but less than 199, marijuana plants is 16."

US v. Graham. 710 F. Supp. 1290, 1291 (ND CAL, April 1989). Opinion and Order, Orrick, District Judge.

"In prosecutions for conspiracy to manufacture and distribute marijuana, if the case involves live marijuana plants, number of plants, rather than their weight, is appropriate measure of amount of marijuana for purposes of sentencing guidelines."

In the October issue of the United States Code An-notated (U.S.C.A.) the issue was addressed again about the weight of marijuana plants.

US v. Miller, 680 F. Supp. 1189
(E.D. Tenn. 1988)

Quantity of Substance

"Weight of marijuana plants stalks was not includable in determining whether weight of marijuana seized subjected defendants to sentence enhancement, where defendants were arrested and marijuana seized at stage before it had been turned into a readily marketable or consumable product."

The abovementioned authorities give me great confidence in knowing that the law is on my side. A wrong has been done, and with your help, I believe it will be corrected.

God bless you!

Sincerely,
David L. Price

Meanwhile, Dell calls the prosecutor. "I happened to see the judge's letter on David Price, and it looks good that he may rule in his favor. What do you think?"

"Oh, no. They just have to do that."

"Oh, they do?"

"Yeah! I mean, it's just a form that they have to take allegations. Tell him not to get his hopes up."

"Is there any way you're going to support it?"

"No! No. There's no way we're going to support it!"

"Well, what's the chance of him getting out during the review process?"

"Slim to none. None."

"Okay, then."

Prosecutor is man with a mission

US prosecutor enjoys his role in drug war

By KATHERINE M. SKIBA
of The Journal staff

His job comes with death threats, middle-of-the-night phone calls and mounds and mounds and mounds of drugs.

R. Jeffrey Wagner, 32, prosecutes narcotics traffickers on behalf of the United States of America, and with considerable success.

Last week, he was the legal brainpower behind the sweep of 30 alleged drug

Soldiers in the war on drugs — the people on the front lines — will be profiled from time to time in The Milwaukee Journal. The profiles will examine the lives of people who work in law enforcement, medicine, rehabilitation and education.

CHAPTER 5

The Retaliation

Cal was right! On the twentieth day from the order to respond, the prosecutor does file a motion for more time.

Three days later (February 19, 1990), Boyle is busy filing a motion to modify Jeffery Dahmer's sentence because of thus:

> 1. a. The defendant (Dahmer) lived with his grandmother before being incarcerated. She is eighty-four years old and has recently slipped and fell, causing her medical condition to deteriorate. Further, that with the winter months, the defendant will again be able to assist his grandmother with his duties around the home and to assist her in her medical condition.
>
> b. The circumstances of the defendant's mental health and changes in his family situation resulting in extreme hardship that can be cured by an appropriate modification of the present incarceration.

2. The defendant has taken positive steps while incarcerated to progress and strive to make a better person of himself. Further, his behavior while incarcerated has been very good, and he has been very cooperative with authorities. Further, the defendant has tremendous remorse for that which has placed him in the institution.

3. That in equity and fairness, the defendant most earnestly pleads for this court to exercise its authority to review and modify its previously imposed sentence.

Gerald P. Boyle
Attorney for Defendant

I wonder what my prosecutor is going to say. I know what I want to say; however, since Cal has hired Stephen Kravit, from Kravit, Waisbren, and DeBruin, I shall write to him.

Dear Mr. Kravit:

First, let me thank you from the bottom of my heart for helping me with my case. I have had no law training whatsoever, and your skills are very much needed and greatly appreciated. I will be to the point. I would like to vacate the conviction more so than the obvious—correction of an illegal sentence. I assert that the court should apply the "cause and prejudice" that's applicable to federal habeas corpus. Boyle's actions with the prosecutor on the agreed-upon weight, inducing me to plead guilty on false information, his refusal of an evidentiary hearing to clarify the issues of fact, his failure to prepare a defense of any kind, his complete failure to inform me of the law relative to the facts of my case (he even admitted to the judge not knowing the law), firmly establish a denial of effective assistance, constituting cause for procedural default, *Murray v. Carrier*, 477 US 478 (1986).

I am very grateful to you and your firm. Please do not take offense from my legal research. My grandfather was a lawyer, and perhaps I have inherited his spirit.

Thank you again,
David L. Price

I go to the chapel. It's peaceful there, and I want God to hear my prayers. There is an elderly inmate called Hoppy who works there. He hands out the free greeting cards to anyone who needs to acknowledge a special occasion. Hoppy is a tall gentleman from Tennessee with a well-trimmed gray-white beard and no mustache. He greets everyone with Southern hospitality. The deep wrinkles across his aging forehead give way to his soft-spoken wisdom and make me feel like I'm talking to Abe Lincoln, a father figure I can confide in.

I explain the latest development with the court ordering the government to respond to my motion. He warns, "Be careful, David. They don't fight fair. I know. I'm being held here, and I still haven't been to court yet, and I've been here for almost four years!"

In shock, I ask, "You mean you haven't been sentenced yet?"

"That's right," he says.

"Did you plead guilty?" I continue to ask.

"No. I am not guilty," he says with a sad, faraway look in his eyes.

"You haven't been to trial?" I probe, still in disbelief.

"That's right. Be careful, David, they're not going to like seeing you win," Hoppy warns.

I've heard stories in the law library about vindictive prosecutors, but Hoppy's case is downright frightening. Am I still in America? *Please, God, I pray for a sign.*

A letter arrives from Social Security explaining that they were contacted by the United States district attorney's office and they are going to suspend my benefits to Penny because I am in prison from a felony for more than one year. At this time, it's been a year since my sentencing, but eight months of actual incarceration. If the court acts in time, this issue could be moot.

February 23, 1990

Hi, Penny!

It is 3:00 a.m., Friday. I cannot sleep, and I am writing to you my thoughts of the recent development in your life. I feel bad, very bad. You are definitely in more of a painful situation than before. It is the darkest before the dawn. I truly believe that I will be home very soon. I will not let anything or anyone do you harm. I am your big protector. You haven't forgotten that, have you? We always said we did not need those checks anyway. They are gone because I am returning to multiply your happiness beyond your fondest dreams.

I am tired of not being with you. I try so hard each day at not becoming angry, hostile, and bitter, and now it's even harder. I hang on to the belief that everything does happen for a reason. It doesn't seem to help when I try to understand, Why is this happening? Penny, nothing can take our love for each other away from us. They have our bodies, but never our souls.

"The weakened mind always see things through a black veil. The soul makes its own horizons!" (Alexander Dumas 1844).

I have enclosed my correspondence to Boyle and to Steve Kravit. I gave it much thought, and I will do whatever Steve says. He is the professional, and he does have our best interest at heart. It wasn't easy, but what it comes down to is *trust*. I have decided that I will give in and turn my affairs over to someone else and trust once again.

It is the same thing when it comes to all our affairs of this life—we must be willing to turn ourselves over to the will of God and trust that he knows best. He can see the end result of the big picture, while we are limited to the vision of the daily brush strokes of life. We are painting a masterpiece, Penny. I really believe that! I will close for now with my prayers for you.

Our new journey through life will begin once we're back together. I love you, Penny. Your joy is my joy; your pain, I can feel, too!

I have your picture on my desk, and I gaze at you with loving affection constantly. Hang in there with me, sweetheart. It will be okay. You'll see.

Goodbye for now, and always keep your chin up and smile for me. I'll make everything up to you. I promise. You'll see. Above all, do not worry. You can always lean on me, Penny.

Forever in your arms,
returning all your love,
David

I place a collect call to the office of Odel Gigante and Associates Limited. They are experts in dealing with administrative law and the

Social Security Administration. The secretary connects me with Del. He explains, "They can't take money away without a hearing." So we formally request a hearing. Then Del points out the law regarding the suspension of benefits.

> Inmate would be given an opportunity to request that a rehabilitation program be approved for him, so as to come within exception to general suspension of benefits. (*Peeler v. Heckler*, 781 F2d (649) [Eighth Circuit 1986])

Del then puts together a motion to order rehabilitation:

> The court erred when they did not order David L. Price into rehabilitation during his incarceration. Further, it is a matter of fact in the record that David could not work, but the court still sent him to a work camp in Duluth, Minnesota.
>
> It has been brought to my attention that his Social Security Disability Benefits are supposed to be discontinued because he has been convicted of a felony. This case is very unusual in that David L. Price's wife has terminal cancer and depends upon the Social Security Disability Benefits to live on, along with her and David's thirteen-year-old daughter. Therefore, we file this motion with the sentencing court, seeking approval of a rehabilitation program. Further, it should be noted here that because he was sentenced to Duluth, where he was forced to perform manual activity, two of the wires broke in his back, close to his spine, and now David is totally dependent upon a cane to ambulate.
>
> Presently, David is in the Rochester Medical Clinic. Doctors have advised him that surgery at

this time would be risky and suggested that he wait for a while before considering surgery to correct the broken-wire problem. With the above in mind, we pray the court will find it benevolent to issue an order for rehabilitation so benefits are not taken away from David's wife and child.

* * * * *

March 1, 1990

Dear Del,

Why does the government want to penalize Penny and Sam? As I see it, this is more evidence that Gerald Boyle did not do his job in representing me. He knew that I was disabled. He knew, or should have known, the law required a suspension *unless* I had the approval of the sentencing court (Reynolds) to become an exception within the statute, so it would have been docketed and there would never have been this hassle put onto Penny.

I called my new lawyer that Cal has hired and asked about this issue. The answer I got was Social Security law is, "Huge and complicated." I feel comfortable with a professional like you, and I want you to know I am grateful to be having you on my side. I spoke with Penny, and she is "wiped out" over everything. I worry about her with the stress she is under in her condition. God bless you for looking after my girl! I want you to know that.

Love ya,
David

Meanwhile, back in Milwaukee, a letter from Medina, Ohio, arrives for Judge William Gardner.

March 1, 1990

Dear Judge Gardner:

I am writing in regard to my son, Jeff Dahmer, who is scheduled to be released from the House of Correction on Tenth Street the first part of March 1990. The reason that I am writing to you is to ask if you would please do what you can to define and maximize the treatment that was mandated in the court record on May 24, 1989.

Ever since May 24, 1989, when I appeared with Jeff and spoke in your courtroom, I have experienced an extremely frustrating time trying to urge initiation of some type of treatment. It was not until almost December 1989 that G. Boyle told me that there existed no coordination of action between your area, his area, and the parole area.

My biggest concern as Jeff is released the first part of this month is, the same situation may ensue that existed in a prior conviction for indecent exposure while intoxicated (approximately 1986 or 1987). Jeff was ordered to obtain therapy for one year with a Dr. Rosen, a woman clinical psychologist. Nine months into the treatment, when I finally was told by Jeff of this treatment, I made a visit to Dr. Rosen. I discovered that she was not a specialist in treating alcoholism and that there were no critical evaluations or feedback to the court or parole people so that changes could be made due to no progress being made in her sessions. Based upon this and several conversations with Jeff's prior generic caseload parole officers, I have tremendous reservations regarding Jeff's chances when he hits the streets.

In closing, every incident, including the most recent conviction for sex offense, has been associated with and initiated by alcohol in Jeff's case. I sincerely hope that you might intervene in some way to help my son, whom I love very much and for whom I want a better life. I think it best to ensure my relationship with Jeff that no one tell him of my efforts toward effective treatment. I do feel, though, that this may be our last chance to institute something lasting and that you hold the key.

Sincerely yours,
Lionel Dahmer

STATE OF WISCONSIN   CIRCUIT COURT   MILWAUKEE COUNTY

STATE OF WISCONSIN,

           Plaintiff,

v.
                      Case No. F-882515

JEFFREY L. DAHMER,

           Defendant.   **16**   *FILED*

MOTION TO MODIFY SENTENCE   FEB 19 1990

                                 CLERK OF COURTS   **16**

To: Milwaukee County District Attorney's Office
       Milwaukee, WI

      NOTICE IS HEREBY GIVEN that the above-named defendant, by and through his attorneys, Gerald P. Boyle, S.C., will move the Honorable Court presided over by William D. Gardner, Circuit Court Judge for Milwaukee County, on the _2nd_ day of _March_ , 1990 at _1 30_ o'clock in the _After_ noon or as soon thereafter as counsel may be heard for entry of an order modifying the previously imposed sentence on the 23rd day of May, 1989 of five (5) years probation with a condition that the first year be served at the House of Correction. The Defendant seeks to be released approximately twenty (20) days prior to his anticipated release from a term of twelve (12) months at the House of Correction as a condition of probation.

      AS GROUNDS THEREFORE, Defendant would show the Court:

      1.   There are new factors which are present which would authorize this Court to exercise discretion in reviewing and modifying the sentence originally imposed. Rosado v. State, 70 Wis.2d 280, 234 N.W.2d 69 (1975).

           a.   That the Defendant lived with his grandmother before being incarcerated; she is 84 years old and has recently slipped and fell causing her medical condition to deteriorate. Further, that with the winter months, the Defendant will again be able to assist his grandmother with his duties around the home and assist her in her medical condition.

b. The circumstances of the Defendant's mental health and changes in his family situation resulting in extreme hardship that can be cured by an appropriate modification of the present incarceration.

2. The Defendant has taken positive steps while incarcerated to progress and strive to make a better person of himself. Further, his behavior while incarcerated has been very good and he has been very cooperative with the authorities. Further, the Defendant has tremendous remorse for that which has placed him in the Institution. Cresci v. State, 89 Wis.2d 495, 278 N.W.2d 850 (1979).

3. That in equity and fairness, the Defendant most earnestly pleads for this Court to exercise its authority to review and modify its previously imposed sentence.

Dated at Milwaukee, Wisconsin this 19th of February, 1990.

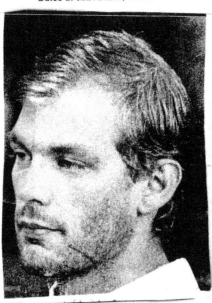

GERALD P. BOYLE, S.C.
Attorneys for Defendant

Gerald P. Boyle
Gerald P. Boyle

Ignoring the concerns of his loving father, and completely forgetting Gail Shelton (the assistant district attorney who prosecuted Dahmer for sexual assault back in 1988) when she testified at his May 23, 1989, sentencing hearing—"The prognosis for treatment within the community is just plain not going to work....His track record exhibits that he is very likely to reoffend."—Judge Gardner releases Dahmer back to Milwaukee's streets anyway. Forget the fact he originally sentenced Dahmer to consecutive five- and three-year terms then stays the sentence and places him on one-year work release from the House of Correction and five years probation. Also, Boyle and Dahmer both signed a form with the court on May 23, 1989, that they would not seek postconviction relief.

Hon. William Gardner Presiding

March 21, 1990, court ordered defendant's condition of probation modified to read "Amount of term served has satisfied the conditions of probation" (defendant released).

In the meantime, back in Rochester, another celebration erupts at mail call. Fred's motion for release pending appeal is granted. I help him pack, and we promise each other to stay in touch. He no longer owns his $600,000 home in Los Angeles, so he will be moving in with his brother Don and continue working on his pro se appeal.

Am I going to be next? I don't think so, if you ask Boyle. He mails a three-page letter to my new lawyer and says thus:

March 16, 1990
Attorney Janice Rhodes
Kravit, Waisbren, and DeBruin
757 N. Broadway
Milwaukee, WI 53202-3612

Dear Ms. Rhodes,

When first contacted by your office about Mr. Price, I went about the business of immediately providing you with everything that I had that was relative to any potential inquiry that another lawyer may wish to make about the case. No one told me what was in the offing or what another lawyer might be looking into, but that mattered not, because whatever Mr. Price wished to do was his business, and if another lawyer wanted documents, such should be immediately provided. Your office did not notify me about what you were looking into for Mr. Price, and frankly, I didn't care one way or the other. I did, however, take it upon myself to send two documents to Mr. Price, for him to turn over to you since they involved fee, which I was sure you weren't looking into, because the Prices still owe my office nine thousand dollars. It was interesting to note, however, that someone who owes my office money was hiring another prestigious law office and, most assuredly, paying a fee for those services. The letter I sent to Mr. Price contained a copy of a letter his wife sent me in November 1988, and I thought it fair that Price send that to you if he wanted to.

Now, I am sending it to you along with a couple or three other cards and notes I found in the file that were not legal in nature but, clearly, might be necessary to dispel some things I found in an affidavit that Mrs. Price filed with some papers her husband filed in January. I learned of that filing yesterday. I read Mrs. Price's affidavit, and it is so preposterous that I thought you might find these little notes she had sent us interesting. For Mrs. Price to now say that we hounded her for money is the most absurd statement imaginable. For her to say that my relationship with Judge Reynolds earlier in life took on some sort of meaning is so insulting that it requires my addressing the same to anyone who wishes to listen. I tell every client I have ever had when I appeared before the Supreme Court that I had the great honor of having been a law clerk to the late Chief Justice Horace Wilkie. I tell every client that I appeared with before Judge Reynolds that earlier in life, I had the privilege of having been on his staff when he was governor as his assistant legal and pardon counsel. I told every client I ever appeared with before the late Judge Hugh R. O'Connell that I had been the deputy district attorney under Hugh when he was the district attorney. I tell clients that because they have a right to know, and I also tell them that my relationship will have no bearing on the case one way or the other except that I am sure the judge involved will listen to what I say because he will respect me just as I respect him. I also make the statement for the simple reason that they may know of my relationships with these men and I don't want them to think that such relationship would have any bearing on the case. Years ago, I discovered that sometimes I was hired or going to be hired because the client or prospective client knew I had this type of prior relationship with the judge in question. I wanted to let them know up front that such relationship meant absolutely nothing in regards to their case. When told this by me, some chose not to hire me, because obviously their motive in hiring me would not have been realized. This type of statement has been made by me to clients for the last twenty years, and this is the first time someone has tried to twist it in a fashion that such as Mrs. Price has. Shame on Mrs. Price. Recently, I was appointed by Judge Landry to be his court commissioner. Rest assured I will tell every client the same thing in regards to Judge Landry. That is just good business, so clients are under any mistaken beliefs. If, after reading the notes sent to me by Mrs. Price, one can still believe that which she says in her affidavit about fee, then I suggest one has blinders on. For Mrs. Price to suggest that her husband wasn't given 110 percent because the total fee wasn't paid is pathetically absurd.

While on vacation last week, I was informed that another letter came in from your office under your signature, asking for file memos, daybooks, calendars, handwritten notes, or whatever. It became clear to me from the content of this letter that something was going on that I wasn't being made aware of. First off, no one told me until I found out from the US attorney's office that some motion existed alleging ineffective assistance. Your earlier correspondence did not allude to that. Your letter of March 7 didn't spell out what you wanted this material for. No lawyer who does this type of work and who has succeeded me in representation has ever asked for the type of things you were asking for. Since I have done about eighty BAPR cases, I thought for a moment that this was a BAPR type of case. The reason I became curious about your request is that wouldn't seem to have a bearing on anything unless you were getting prepared to defend Mr. Price on a fee contest case. But now I am informed that you talked with my associate telephonically and told him the story of your involvement with Mr. Price.

I care not that Mr. Price has filed the motion that he had raised, including this nonsense about the ineffective assistance business. Frankly, I don't really care that Mrs. Price has signed an affidavit that is patently absurd, and I really don't care that your office is looking into this matter, but I do care that I am not informed as to why you want material such as you asked for in your March 7 letter. If I had been so informed, I could have given you an easy response to your inquiry.

Knowing that your superior, Steve Kravit, is an experienced defense attorney, and believing that you understand the nature and extent of the business of being a defense attorney in cases such as Mr. Price's, it is my hope that you will understand that attorneys such as myself did not file memos to the file, nor do we keep handwritten notes except as needed. We had volumes of materials on Mr. Price. We filed extensive motions on his behalf. We had numerous meetings with him and his wife. There was no reason to keep the kinds of things you were seeking. We knew when we were to meet him. We knew when he would be coming into our office. We knew when we had to be in court with him. There is no way you will be seeing my daybooks or calendars. If you want to know when we talked to him in the office, we'll try to reconstruct that. If you want to know when he called us, we'll try to reconstruct that. When we were in court with him is a matter of record in the file. If you're trying to suggest that we didn't spend much time with Mr. Price, then make that suggestion and we'll respond in kind. Your request for our work product without informing us as to why you want it is a little disconcerting, but suffice it to say, Mr. Price's file memos are one and the same as the motions that were filed on his behalf. I just can't visualize the kind of file memos that one might expect to find in a case of this kind. Were Mr. Steinle and I expected to write notes to each other when most of the time we were together talking with the Prices or discussing the case between us? Such, at least up to now, has not been the nature of my practice. We weren't charging him an hourly fee, so there wasn't much reason to keep those kinds of informational things for billing purposes.

When I returned, I found the enclosed cards and also a letter I received from another lawyer about this dried-weight business. I don't know if that was already sent to you or not, but it demonstrates that this grasping at straws that Mr. Price is doing has little, if any, merit.

I just want to make it clear that Mr. Price is perpetuating a fraud if he is trying to accuse my associate and me of not properly representing him. He knew full well about the weight business. Mr. Steinle can attest to that, as can Mr. Wagner. Also, Mr. Price knew what he was facing if he wished to challenge the charges.

I couldn't have cared less if he wanted to go to trial. But Mr. Price wanted the best possible deal he could get. His promises of cooperation were finally only that, just promises. Time and again, he kept on saying he was afraid of cooperating because of fear for his life, etc. Not an uncommon occurrence, this business of fear, but his failure to cooperate kept him from going out of the guidelines. He got the minimums in the guidelines and had the minimum mandatory sentence count dismissed, plus all the other counts and other things the US attorney could have done short of a plea were estopped. His tunnel vision about this dried-weight business is a little after the fact. He joined in the stipulation. His claim that Mr. Steinle didn't do his job is insulting. Their statements about me are just out-and-out garbage. The true character of the Prices are now highlighted. I am told they were unsuccessful in this civil claim that was going to result in compensation to my office. So be it, but I can assure you the only reason I did not get out of the case way back when was that I felt Mr. and Mrs. Price were honorable people who meant what they said personally to Mike Steinle and me and what they stated in their letters. I have been fooled before, and I'll be fooled again, but since everyone has to live with their conscience, I can only say I'm glad I don't have to live with the Prices' conscience.

Do what you have to do. What you have received is what there is. I have rescrutinized my file in view of your last letter and am responding to what you asked for.

Believe me, I am not sensitive as to what you are doing. I would have appreciated an earlier explanation, and certainly would have expected one in your letter of March 7, but in view of your phone call to Mike Steinle, and now that I know about this motion Price has filed, I can now safely say I understand what everyone is doing and I will do what is appropriate under the circumstances. If there is more that you need, let us know.

Sincerely yours,
Gerald P. Boyle

I'm not going home according to the government either! Their response to the court is predictably out-of-context quotes, irrelevant case law, and boldfaced prevarications.

The judge now refers my case to "United States Magistrate Robert L. Bittner to conduct any hearings necessary and issue his recommendation to the court."

If that isn't bad enough, Social Security decides (without a hearing) to suspend benefits to Penny and claim she fraudulently accepted $8,846!

Now she is unable to pay her medical insurance premium, which, as of last month, has almost tripled.

A letter from Penny arrives on March 19, 1990.

Hi, Dave!

It is Monday night, and I am watching the Fourth Annual American Comedy Awards. It is pretty funny. I always like to laugh. I don't enjoy being sad or mad or, worse yet, depressed, so I decided to shake the bad feelings. I guess I should reverence the simple things.

You have told me many times what we think about eventually does happen. To be honest, that is where I get my enthusiasm. When I think about your freedom, it makes me happy. I refuse to give up. I truly do believe it will be reality. Do you still dream of our life together? What do you think is going to happen? We do have a lot of love between us, and that is all that matters. Although we are apart, we are still building a life together.

I want you to know I trust our new attorneys. It isn't easy, but we can't judge all attorneys as the kind of attorney Boyle and Steinle were. It's always hard to put our lives in someone else's control. However, this time, you are protecting our interests. Cal has excellent judgment, and he has selected Steve, so I will put my faith in Steve, Cal, Janice, Dell, and of course, you. You have always come through for me. Thank you. I want you to know how grateful I am for your taking care of me and standing with me. I sincerely appreciate your work in the law and finding the strength to keep me going. I guess there are times I'm not as strong as I would like to be.

I have been doing a lot of thinking about Cal. He is on my mind a lot. I have a feeling it is because of Nana that he has come to our rescue. You are a wise man. I am very proud of you. Nana is smiling that I have you. I do know how lucky I am to have you for my other half. I have a lot to be thankful for. You have always taken care of me; even with your being in prison, you are still taking pains for me. Your foresight gives me encouragement. I believe in your promises. I believe in you. Our freedom from prison and poverty is not far away. I love you.

I have to tell you, Dave, you give me hope and inspiration for our future. You truly multiply my happiness. I don't believe that puts too much pressure on you. You are capable of abundance in everything you do. God's spirit is all about you all day long.

I was happy you made the decision not to answer Boyle's letter. Boyle is the kind of person I simply don't trust. I try to follow the Baha'i writings of always looking for beauty of character in those around us, but Boyle is a difficult character to find good in. I can't help but wonder what Steve and Janice think of Boyle.

Dell stopped by last night. He dropped off some forms for us to fill out. I will send them to you tomorrow. He wants me to let him read Jeff's response. I promised to drop off the copy I have from Steve. I have to admit that at first, the government's memorandum (Jeff's response) to your motion for writ of habeas corpus frightened me. But now you have pointed out how Jeff is not right. I have all my trust in you and Steve and Janice to set the record straight and get you out. I want you back with me. This life apart is for the birds.

I can't tell you enough how proud I am for your desire in learning the law. You are a natural for it. Actually, you are a natural for whatever you set out to do. There is no limit to what you can do. You have always been a man of many talents. But somehow I can't help but feel, ever since your prison experience, you have developed a special character about you. It's like when the soul finds its home of rest in God, then it is that real life begins. Our real life is about to begin.

It's no surprise to me that Steve and Janice want your input. You are right about a lot of things, and your persistence in studying the law is making you a benefit. You know the way things happened better than anyone else. I know that you continue to amaze me every day. I am grateful for your calmness and persistence. You couldn't have said it better when you wrote me, "When it comes to anything that concerns our well-being, I will always put my input into it and not accept someone else's belief that I cannot contribute." It's great to hear you believe in yourself like you do. See how lucky I am to have you. How many wives have a special man like I do? Not very many, and I am thanking God and you every day of my life. You keep me going! There is no one like you. You are truly a very spiritual, good person. You are my sweetheart! No one can make me feel like the way you make me feel.

Forever loving you today,
tomorrow, and always,
your wife,
Penny

I need to see Penny. I want to hold her tight and kiss her gently and reassure her everything will be all right.

When they enter the visiting room, I hug 'em both at the same time. God, I miss them! As we sit at a table in the visitor's room, Samantha keeps staring at the lady sitting and crying at the table next to us. It is Tammy Faye Bakker, and her makeup is running all over her tear-soaked face. I must admit, I can't blame Sammie for staring. We get up and go outside to the visitor's pen. I'm trying to tell Penny about all the inmates drinking hydrogen peroxide, but she doesn't want to hear it. She still has faith in her surgery and radiation, and I don't want to take that away from her. Penny is more concerned about me and the legal developments looming on the horizon.

Our goodbyes are so hard. I can't stand all the suffering my two girls are going through. This is *not* how God intends it to be.

CHAPTER 6

The Jailhouse Lawyer

Garry tries to cheer me up. He writes to the Recreation Department, "We, Garry McClain and David Price, would very much like to be considered for a garden plot. We are both medical patients from the 10-1 unit, and in our limited capacity, we will do our utmost best to exhibit a vegetable display that would more accurately reflect the treatment and therapy of the Recreation Department. However, we aren't promising you a rose garden." Nevertheless, we now have a garden. It's four feet wide and twelve feet long, staked and numbered along with thirty-nine others.

I've been so wrapped up in the law library. I need to get away. I need to trust in God and my new lawyers. The garden plot is just what I need. Sitting in the grass and watching our tomatoes, hot peppers, pickles, and onions grow brings me back to God's will.

I have time on my hands, and I still can't stay away from the law books. I now find myself interviewing inmates, taking notes, researching applicable law, and typing up the paperwork that they need. I begin to be the voice of many. What I'm finding is that I'm not the only one with a problem with the justice system. I will do what I can, God willing.

The person I want to help most is my friend Garry, whose health is rapidly declining. Here is his motion for modification of term or reduction of sentence mailed to the United States District Court, Eastern District of Kentucky.

Comes now Garry McClain, pro se defendant, pursuant to and in accordance with the provisions of Title 18, United States Code Section(s) 3582 (c) and 3553 (a), (b) and (e), and respectfully moves the court for an order granting him a modification of the term of imprisonment or reduction of the sentence imposed May 5, 1989. In support of this motion, defendant states:

1. Defendant seeks a modification of the sentence imposed by the court for both compelling and extraordinary circumstances. Defendant's medical condition relevant to the serious instabilities of his heart may be fatal before the sentence expires. A heart specialist, Dr. E. Singer of University Hospital, Louisville, Kentucky, has stated in his report that defendant has a deteriorating heart condition, malignant ventricular tachycardia refractory to medical therapy. He also has had a ventricular scar resected and an automatic implantable defibrillator placed in 1987. Since that time, defendant has had the automatic defibrillator replaced due to the malfunction of the first implant. At that time, the automatic defibrillator was not FDA approved, and defendant had volunteered to test-case the new device so it would someday be able to help save lives in the future. He further volunteered for an untested and unapproved new drug, amiodarone, which is an antiarrhythmic drug. The defendant also suffers from coronary artery disease, which enhances a negative diagnosis. (See Exhibit A.)

2. Defendant is incarcerated far away from his wife and children, which compounds his stress and strain and, of course, magnifies his chance of heart failure. In addition, the treatment and care received at the federal facilities is not as effective and as adequate as he can receive on an outpatient basis in the community. Also, defendant has been told by a physician that there is a fifty-fifty chance that he will not live long enough to complete the sentence imposed by the court. Defendant notes that he is not given the careful and concerned type of treatment needed from the confines of an institution. He is required to have constant checkups of the device (defibrillator) and regular checks of his lungs, eyes, kidneys, and skin from the adverse affects of amiodarone, however, is not being done as would be expected. Incarceration of the defendant, continued in the custody of the attorney general, could result in his death or, if not so, imminently facilitate and worsen his heart condition whereas shortening the period of time left for him to live. The sword of justice, as necessary for the court to use in protecting the public and punishing those whose actions threaten the welfare and safety of the community, need not be used absent of magnanimity and inconsiderate of the circumstances. The court has discretion and is empowered under the Sentencing Guidelines in placing defendant in community custody, section 5F5.1(a). For the court's consideration, in showing defendant's willingness to be of a substantial benefit to the community and obvious unselfishness, he volunteered himself to be subjected to experimental programs, in response to

being asked, "If it will benefit others, I'll do it," as was previously articulated.

3. The government agreed that the defendant reserved the right to bring to the attention of the sentencing court any and all relevant evidence in mitigation of the offense (see Plea Agreement, Exhibit B). Defendant was helpful to the government and public in apprehension of a drug dealer whose harm to society was substantial. On May 5, 1988, in a federal criminal prosecution, defendant's cooperation with authorities resulted in the conviction and sentence of a Robert Ward to ninety-seven (97) months. Pursuant to the Sentencing Guidelines Section, 5kl.1 or 18 USC Section 3553(e) (see *United States v. Curran*, 724 F. Supp. 1239 [CD ILL 1989]).

After considering the policy statement in Section 5kl.1, the district court may depart from the guideline sentencing range and impose either a more lenient or more severe sentence (citing 18 USC Section 3553[b], *United States v. Scroggins*, 880 F.2d 1201, 1210 [11th Cir. 1989]). Further, this motion should be held cognizable before the court on a due process requirement, although the rule "seems" to require the prosecution to lodge such a motion, if stringently applied, violates the fundamental aspects of due process in this instance. The right to be heard on the issue of a sentencing modification is well settled, Curran, id. at 1242-44. Notwithstanding, judges have the power to make their own decisions about rewarding cooperation and considering a departure may not require a motion by the government (emphasis added),

United States v. Justice, 877 F.2d 664, 699 (8th Cir. 1989). It's the court's inherent judicial function under article III of the Constitution to grant a reduction of sentence where appropriate, *United States v. Smith*, 686 F. Supp. 847, 870 (D. Colo. 1988). And the authority upon which this motion for reduction is explicitly authorized and within "the sentencing judge's discretion," *United States v. Myers*, 687 F. Supp. 1403, 1419 (N. D. Cal. 1988).

4. Defendant has well demonstrated that he can be responsible and has met the requirements on the issue of giving substantial assistance of real value in a criminal prosecution that resulted in the conviction of a drug dealer. He respectfully asks the court to consider him of value and as well as his life in the same. He is more than willing to do community service, to use his experience to teach others the treachery of which drugs has done to his life and others'. He is willing to volunteer his service and will abide by the most strict conditions of community custody that the court might deem proper.

Wherefore, defendant respectfully moves the court for an order granting him consideration on the issue above raised and grant him a reduction of sentence based on the compelling and extraordinary circumstances presented.

The ninth day of April 1990.

Respectfully submitted,
Garry McClain

As Garry reads and signs his motion, you can actually see a glimmer of hope in his eyes. Now Garry, too, is one who waits to hear back from the court. I hope it works for him; however, we must be prepared to reply to the government's response, so I remain in the law library.

Joe Geniola is a hard man not to like. The ring of hair over his ears and around his head below the bald top gives him the impression of a clown. His large frame is accompanied with an equally deep laugh, which he practices quite frequently. Joe is transferred here from Sandstone. He finds that his good time credit is not up-to-date for his parole hearing, which is coming up. Every little bit of time reduced means a lot when you are Joe's age, which is over sixty.

The parole hearing for Joe goes bad. I type up a request for the parole hearing tape so I can listen, transcribe, and then put together his appeals.

Ground 1: The guidelines were incorrectly applied as to the Offense Severity Rating.

At the parole hearing, appellant (Joe) was rushed through in approximately ten (10) minutes because they were running late. Appellant did not get the chance to rebut their information, nor did he get the opportunity to present court documents that support an offense severity less than the six (6) rating determined by the board.

The Parole Board contends that appellant belonged to an organization that extorted over one million dollars. Appellant did not belong to an organization that extorted that kind of money. Granted, appellant was found guilty of committing four (4) predicate acts to extort money. It is interesting to note that in one of them, the only money was one hundred dollars a week for three (3) weeks. In another, no money whatsoever, nor was there ever any threat or implied violence, yet he was convicted of "conspiracy" to extort. The main thrust in the conviction of appellant was that he was a gambler who ran parlay sheets for the football season. He was not a leader, organizer, or kingpin, and the government acknowledges such. Appellant did not belong to an organization that extorted the kind of money alleged.

The Honorable David G. Larimer, US district judge for the Western District of New York, has stated, "Certain other material raised by the government, I think, presents a relevance problem in my view, and therefore I decline to consider it, since I think the law is clear that if the conduct does not relate directly to the defendant, he can't be punished for the activities of others." (Sentencing Tr. p. 9.)

Further, the court found that evidence is clear that appellant was never involved with the codefendants in their past. He was only involved as part of the parlay sheet operation.

In concluding, appellant's guideline range was originally calculated as 24 to 36 months based on a severity rating of five (5). Appellant is asking the commission to reconsider in light of the new evidence and the facts in their proper perspective, the offense severity rating.

Ground 2: The decision was based on erroneous information, and the actual facts justify a different decision.

In the presentence investigation (PSI), the government mentions the criminal activity of the last twenty years of others and infers that appellant was a part of. Appellant was/is not a part of that criminal past, and after a lengthy trial, he was vindicated from it.

I do not think I can attribute that criminal conduct, based on what's in the memorandum, to Mr. Geniola. Again, the cases are pretty clear that you cannot ascribe criminal conduct to even associates of the defendant without showing that he participated, directed, or condoned that activity, so if I have to make a specific finding here, I do, and that is that particular matter will not be taken into account at sentencing because I don't think I can. (Sentencing Tr. p. 11)

Since there are multiple codefendants in a trial atmosphere, the writer of appellant's PSI has confused the facts of a complicated case. The judge, after reviewing the tapes and the testimony, corrected the record at the sentencing court, and appellant offers it to the commission as Exhibit A.

Reliance on erroneous statements in the PSI can hold no weight. The Parole Commission's own rules prohibit the commission from treating the PSI as an unassailable source of factual information (Parole Commission Rules, 2.19-OMp 25).

Appellant is over sixty years old. He has no prior arrest record whatsoever. He has been a life-long resident of Rochester, New York, employed for the past thirty years, and a union member with the Teamsters. He has an excellent work record and a strong parole plan when he gets home. He is known around the community for displaying good character.

Appellant is very sorry for what he has done. He is humbly asking the commission to consider

this appeal and treat his crime in the guideline
category it rightfully belongs.

Respectfully submitted,
Joe Geniola

Roy Kappen is a sixty-five-year-old farmer from Bayard,
Nebraska. He was the town chairman and the owner of three farms.
He rented the house on farm number 3 to people he didn't know
who said they were from Minnesota. They had planted marijuana in
his cornfield under the central pivot irrigation system. Reacting on a
"tip," the police stormed Roy's farm. What they find was Roy on his
tractor, doing chores, the tenants gone (moved away in the middle of
the previous night), and marijuana in his cornfield. Roy doesn't even
know what a marijuana plant looks like.

I, Roy Kappen, being duly sworn and under
oath according to the laws of the United States,
deposes and states thus:

1. I am the affiant, and I make this sworn affidavit under oath and subject to the penalties of
perjury under the laws of the United States.

2. In November 1987, I hired Kirk E. Naylor to
represent me in the above-captioned criminal
matter.

3. I paid him $10,000 in advance, to be worked
out at the rate of $85.00 per hour, in repre-
senting me in the abovementioned case.

4. Attorney Naylor persuaded me to plead guilty
by indicating to me that if I should continue
to maintain my innocence and go to trial, I

would get "butchered" and receive ten (10) years to life without parole. He also said that the government had information that he did not have. In addition, he promised me that if I would plead guilty, I would receive no more than two (2) years and, with my standing in the community, I should get probation and the government would not take our (320-acre) farm, due to the plea bargain. Instead, I got fifteen (15) years, and now the government is trying to take our farm.

5. I did not have any opportunity to discuss the "presentence investigation report" with Mr. Naylor. He gave me a copy of the report to read and sign ten (10) minutes before we went to court. He never explained or discussed the importance of this document and the factual inaccuracies contained therein.

6. I signed a document entitled "Petition to Enter Plea of Guilty," which was accepted by the court on July 1, 1988, which was also signed by the prosecutor and my attorney. Question number 17(c) specifically asks, "Will you be forfeiting any property to the United States as a result of your guilty plea? No.!" It was my understanding that this promise was/is binding. Further, in regards to question number 45, my attorney (Naylor) advised me that I had a good chance to get probation, "considering [my] clean record," and that I should tell them what they wanted to hear. He typed the entire document in my absence and had me sign it on his advice.

7. I am presently incarcerated in Rochester Federal Medical Center, and I am temporarily separated from all my legal material and personal property.

8. I was given an extension by the court to file this affidavit and hereby request I be allowed to finish officially informing the court by way of another affidavit when my property arrives from FPC Yankton, South Dakota.

Respectfully submitted,
Roy Kappen

An inmate from the weight room, with muscles bulging out his tattoos, comes over to me sitting in the law library. He has his parole hearing tape and wants my help. I listen to the tape and comment, "Gosh. You'd a thought you killed somebody!"

His reply was a callous "I did."

I hand him back his tape and say, "I don't have time for people who do that."

He returns to the gym to lift more weights.

Sid Mayley is next. He has been in prison so long I think he has forgotten what he's in here for. Anyway, Sid wants a request for administrative remedy typed up for his smoking problems:

I am requesting to be treated the same as the inmates in buildings 1 and 2. These inmates are allowed to smoke in their cells. The staff and general population inmates are allowed to smoke in building 10; however, we inmates in 10-1 and 10-2 are prohibited. Why aren't we allowed? This is clearly an act of discrimination and a direct violation of 1640.2A Institution Supplement Smoking and No Smoking Areas.

(5)(a) "Smoking areas will be clearly identi-
fied for staff and inmates."

By making a clear overall, general smoke-
free program for the entire population of the 10-1
and 10-2 units and without taking into consideration the individuals' needs by the unit team
is a direct violation of Institution Supplement
Nondiscrimination Towards Inmates.

(5) "All inmates will be reviewed for...pro-
grams by their unit team. It will be the responsibility of the unit team to assist in developing a
program for the inmate based upon his needs."

I request to be treated for the physical
addiction caused from smoking. The administration treats people for drug and alcohol addic-
tions. Why won't you treat the physical addiction
of smoking? I don't need an inmate-run program
to show me pictures; I can look in the mirror. I
further request that program statement 1640.2
be made available to the inmate population.

Sid Mayley
April 17, 1990

I get a letter from Fred today.

April 26, 1990

Dear Dave:

I thought I'd better write a letter to let you know
how things are going. First of all, I've heard from
two sources that we won our case in the appeals
court, but we don't have any official word yet.
A few weeks ago, my attorney called the public

defender (a guy by the name of Mike Harris and whom we got to know quite well during trial) in Kansas City, Kansas. He, in turn, had talked to our judge's law clerk, who had told him that the case had been overturned. Also, we heard that the federal prosecutor in our case, a Lloyd Monroe (who quit the Justice Department last July), called the investigative reporter with the *Houston Post*, Pete Brewton, and evidently was very angry and upset because he (Monroe) had heard that the case was overturned. So I sit here day to day and wait for the official word.

Regarding my health, I seem to be doing okay, but let me go into a little more detail. Shortly after coming home, I saw my urologist (Dr. Greenberg), the same person who had treated me in 1985 and 1986 and followed up since. He proceeded to give me some gloomy predictions, and he hadn't even received any report from PMC yet. Anyway, he asked me to come back a month or so later and he would study the matter some more. I also went to see my general practitioner, Dr. Coleman, to talk to him about the operation as well as the high calcium count, which they considered a problem at FMC, although not a serious one. He took a blood test, wherein just about everything was measured. The calcium count was now down to 11. In FMC, they had measured 11.6 (normal should be 7.5 to 10). More importantly, Dr. Coleman told me, "You apparently have that tumor thing well under control." The cholesterol was 167. At FMC, they had measured 159.

I was then back for the second appointment with Dr. Greenberg. He said I looked better than the first visit, with better flesh color, etc. Nevertheless, he wanted me to be examined by a Dr. Boyd at the USC Norris Cancer Center, a very respected place. I went there, talked to Dr. Boyd, and had a CAT scan taken. He felt in my right groin and said that he could feel the lymph node (but that's true with everybody), but he also thought it was only slightly enlarged. A couple of days later, the CAT scan showed nothing in that area, just like the two CAT scans had shown at the Mayo.

In early March, I was back to Dr. Coleman for a second blood test. This time, my calcium count was down to 10.6, an improvement, but still a way to go. The cholesterol had now crept up to 18—nothing to worry about, though. Most important, a cancer measurement, CEA, was 1 (normal is 0.5 to 2). At this point, I'm still on peroxide, supplemented with some SOD-3.

The next step was that a nutritional expert, a Dr. Shoden (not an MD), was highly recommended to me. He works in conjunction with a Dr. La. Senla (sp?), a retired MD (I'm told he used to be Ronald Regan's private doctor), and who is also into alternative treatments. Anyway, Dr. Shoden primarily looks in detail at your blood. He takes a drop of blood and spreads it out on a small glass plate, sticks it under a 400X microscope, and you can actually see the red and white blood cells. Now, in spite of the fact that the standard blood test was extremely satisfactory, Dr. Shoden could see where the red blood cells were bunching together, whereas they should be swimming around freely.

He then prescribes a whole series of nutrient additives to build up the immune system. And I agree with him; in order to fight cancer and many other illnesses, the immune system needs to be as healthy as possible. On my second visit to Dr. Shoden, there was a marked improvement in the spreading of the red blood cells. I had my third visit just over a week ago, and it looked better yet. In the meantime, Dr. Boyd has recommended chemotherapy and another operation, something I'm just not very interested in. The thing is, there is no proof that there is anything wrong. I just think the doctors want to cut to make their big fees.

By the way, when I came home, I had to have a new driver's license. Thus, I now have a picture of what I looked like in late January. I showed this picture to Dr. Coleman some two months after I came home. He said, "You look fifteen years younger now." I figure I must be doing something right.

You might also like to know, by the way, that my lawyer has now started some cause of action against the Justice Department and the BOP for allowing the cancer to grow in the first place.

On a whole different subject, I remember seeing some legal citation on the subject of pro se. These citations addressing themselves to the issue, that pro se litigants must be given every reasonable benefit of the doubt in their presentation, arguments, and such. I checked with my codefendant, who was at the Leavenworth Camp, but he doesn't remember that. I've looked for that in the local law library here but haven't located anything on it. Maybe you can inquire into that with somebody at the law library there. I'd appreciate it very much.

I hope you have made some progress in your own case so that you may be home soon. It certainly seems to me that the old judge in your case didn't know what he was doing. Your lawyer was no help either.

With all good wishes,
Fred Figge
16112 Maidstone Ave.
Norwalk, CA 90650

PS: My mother-in-law flew back to Copenhagen a couple of weeks ago.

"Fred won! Can you believe it? He got his conviction over-turned!" I yell across the room at mail call.

"Yes! Yes! Damn them bastards anyway!" cries out Garry with his fists clenched like a prizefighter.

"It sure feels good knowing they don't always win," I say, thinking about my own case situation.

Hoppy reminds us, "And they don't fight fair."

A small thin older gentleman, his graying hair combed straight back, arm stained with an aged WWII tattoo, face covered with white stubble, walks with an air of dignity toward me and asks, "Will you help me?"

"I'll do my best, Albert."

Albert Rush (plaintiff) is a sixty-five-year-old grandpa who is fighting in court against the prison staff (the defendants) for his Rolex watch back.

Comes now Albert E. Rush, pro se plaintiff in the above-entitled action, respectfully moves the court for an order denying defendant's motion to dismiss and enter an order for continuance to permit affidavits to be obtained, pursuant to Rule 56(f), Federal Rules of Criminal Procedure. In support, plaintiff states as follows:

1. On December 21, 1989, plaintiff received an incoming package from home. The items were inventoried by M. J. Pischke and recorded on an institution document called Inmate Personal Property Record (Exhibit A). This document was filled out in its entirety by M. J. Pischke, including the initials AR and the *x* by the box claiming no individual item over $100. A review of the document will show that the initials A and R were made in the same handwriting as the person who filled out the top portion of the form and in no way resemble the handwriting of the plaintiff. Plaintiff did not initial this statement. Plaintiff only signed by the "acknowledging reviewing the property returned." In no way did plaintiff acknowledge that no item of personal property excceded $100 in value, as Ms. Pischke alleges in her declaration. A close examination of the initials A and R in Exhibit A will show that they are not plaintiff's but belong to the officer who filled out the form. Officer Pischke forged plaintiff's initials on the document acknowledging no item exceeded $100 in value. The contents of the box that the watch arrived in were not opened for inspection by Officer

Pischke. Indeed, Had the box been opened that contained the Rolex watch, both parties would have recognized a Rolex watch. Ms. Pischke implying that plaintiff acknowledged that no item of personal property exceeded $100 in value is false and is intended to mislead the court. Ms. Pischke did not do her job of inventorying according to BOP policy. Had she done so, the Rolex watch would have been discovered and she would not have had to hide behind Institutional Supplement 5580.2 to cover up her incompetence. Officer Pischke should be held in contempt for lying and misleading the court and subjected to the penalties of perjury.

2. On December 25, 1989, plaintiff's Rolex watch was confiscated by Officer Dilley and Lieutenant Thomas Peterson, who, in turn, gave plaintiff a Confiscation and Disposition of Contraband receipt (Exhibit B). Lieutenant Peterson told plaintiff, "I'll give you eight five for it." To which plaintiff replied, "Man, there ain't no way I'd take eighty five (85) for it!" Lieutenant Peterson responded, "I mean eight five *big ones*! Believe me, I know what that watch is worth. I have a partner who has a jewelry store, and I know what that watch is worth!" Then Officer Dilley consoled plaintiff, "You don't want to wear that watch around here. Somebody would knock you in the head and steal it. The cheapest Rolex that they make starts at thirty-five to thirty-eight hundred dollars." These two men were aware of the value of the Rolex watch and, with the

desire to own it, expressed a motive for securing its possession.

3. From the time of the December 25 confiscation to January 19, 1990, plaintiff sought on several occasions an administrative remedy (BP-9) from Ms. Pischke to formally protest the fact that the watch was being held. Each time, Ms. Pischke would deny plaintiff the BP-9 and would instead attempt to resolve the matter informally. Finally, on January 19, 1990, plaintiff was allowed to mail the watch home. On that day, Ms. Pischke and plaintiff packed the Rolex watch in a box and attached a handwritten certified mail receipt, not a typed one, as exhibited by the defendants in their Exhibit 2, from M. J. Pischke. Plaintiff has yet to receive the original green postcard receipt; however, the court was given a poor, darkened photocopy of a postcard with a typed label on it in place of the original handwritten one. This was purposely done so as to obscure the post mark from the post office that would prove that defendants had, from January 19 to February 12, wanted to pilfer the Rolex watch. In addition, defendants submitted a copy of the certified mail receipt so light that, again, the court cannot see the official stamp from the post office. This is a deceptive technique and is done only to hinder the court from ascertaining the truth! Plaintiff now submits a clear copy of the certified mail receipt (Exhibit D), and defendants should be charged with yet another act of criminal contempt.

4. On January 19, 1990, plaintiff, at the time of addressing the watch, inquired with the two men (Anderson and Loftness) who work in the postal room about how many stamps it would take to insure the watch. Anderson's comment was, "Naw, he can't insure it!" Plaintiff pleaded with Loftness, and Loftness, in return, questioned Anderson again, to which he remarked, "You can't insure that! Besides, you've certified it and it will be logged at every post office." These two men work in the postal room every day. Inmates do not request packages be insured every day. Anderson and Loftness both quite unconvincingly "don't recall." The court is asked to review the declarations of these two men. Plaintiff specifically discussed insuring his package, and they both were involved in the discussion of the package. Now, why are they both hiding behind the defense of "I don't recall"? unless they are both involved in the conspiracy to pilfer plaintiff's Presidential Rolex watch, known to be worth many thousands of dollars!

5. Also, on January 19, 1990, plaintiff then went straight to Unit Manager Calabrese, and in the unit office lounge, in front of witness James Lay, plaintiff asked about insuring his watch. Mr. Calabrese said, "I never heard of anything being insured leaving this institution!" Plaintiff seeks an affidavit from the witness James Lay, who was present and heard Mr. Calabrese deny knowledge of insuring packages. The very day, plaintiff came from

the mail room after trying unsuccessfully to insure his watch. Mr. Calabrese is caught in two misrepresentations with the court. He stated in his declaration to the court that plaintiff came to him weeks after mailing his package when, in fact, it was the same day as the mailing (January 19, 1990) and that he was not familiar with insuring packages leaving the institution.

6. Mr. Daryl Kosiak, BOP attorney for the institution, has declared that plaintiff did not file a federal tort claim for the loss of his property. This is untrue. Plaintiff submits as Exhibit E a copy of the tort claim that was filed on February 22, 1990, with thus:

C, Bf Faulkner, Regional Counsel
Federal Bureau of Prisons
10920 Ambassador Dr. Suite 220
Kansas City, MO 6153

Kosiak's contention that plaintiff did not file a tort claim must be rejected. To further support plaintiff's position, a tort claim filed on December 9, 1989, was not acknowledged by the BOP until April 30, 1990 (Exhibit F). It appears the government affords itself six (6) months in which to process a federal tort claim. So plaintiff's February 22, 1990, tort claim will quite possibly not surface until sometime in July of 1990.

7. Plaintiff seeks the affidavit of Bonita Jackson along with photocopies of her phone bill to verify the fact that plaintiff phoned on

January 20, 1990, to be expecting his Rolex watch via certified mail. Plaintiff was led to believe by defendants that his Rolex was safely certified and mailed. For approximately twenty-eight (28) days, plaintiff suffered with the torment and agony of the whereabouts of the gift from the son he had lost. The gift of a Presidential Rolex watch. Not just a watch, but a family heirloom. When the package finally did arrive to Bonita (daughter), the box contained a cheap plastic Timex! Plaintiff still grieves to this day, not only the fact that this priceless jewel is gone, but also the way it was taken from him. The deception, the lies, and the downright uncooperative, uncaring attitude of a group of professionals that took advantage of their positions of power and abused a sixty-five-year-old man.

Argument of Law

A. Prison officials violated plaintiff's constitutional rights by refusing to mail plaintiff's package to his daughter.

The Fourth Amendment of the United States Constitution guarantees citizens of the United States the absolute right to be free from unreasonable searches and seizures carried out by virtue of federal authority, *Bivens v. Six Unknown Fed. Narcotics Agents*, 403 US 388 at 392 (1971). Plaintiff's watch was seized and unlawfully detained by defendants. Prison officials are being judicially required to justify such actions, *McNamara v. Moody*, 606 F.2d 621 (Fifth Circuit

1979). Bivens liability is created when federal officers violate a citizen's protected right.

"Where Federally protected rights have been invaded, it has been the rule from the beginning that courts will be alert to adjust their remedies so as to grant the necessary relief," citing *Bell v. Hood*, 327 U. at 684, 90 L. Ed at 944 (footnote omitted).

The contention by defendants that plaintiff has failed to state a claim must be rejected. Plaintiff has a constitutional right to be free from infringements of constitutional rights by federal officers, and the court has jurisdiction over such disputes, *Patmore v. Carlson*, 392 F. Supp. 737 (DC Ill. 1975). When federal officers abuse their position and violate the Constitution, plaintiff's claim need not be proven to establish jurisdiction, *Foster v. Tourtelotte*, 7004 F.2d 1109 (Ninth Circuit 1983). In addition, federal personnel who have deprived a person of his constitutional rights can be sued for damages and other relief under Bivens, *Faverweather v. Bell*, 447 F. Supp. 913, 916 (DC Pa. 1978). Plaintiff's Presidential Rolex watch was deprived from his person without due process. Plaintiff had repeatedly requested administrative remedy and was denied from filing by Ms. Pischke and had stated a cause of action, *Grissom v. Roanoke County*, 348 F. Supp. 321 (DC Va. 1972).

B. Complaint should not be dismissed for failure to state a claim.

Plaintiff has a limited education and is untrained at law and shouldn't be held to the stringent standards of lawyers, *Haynes v. Kerner*, 404 US 519 at 520 (1972).

Wherefore, plaintiff, Albert E. Rush, pro se, respectfully moves this court for an order for a continuance to submit affidavits in support of his claim and deny the defendant's motion to dismiss and grant summary judgment.

Respectfully submitted,
Albert E. Rush
pro se plaintiff
Reg. No. 88179-132
Post Office Box 4600
Rochester, MR 55903

I sit and watch Hoppy read Albert's motion. I am eager to hear his reaction. When he finishes, the bifocals drop from his nose and hang from his neck. He gets up and walks to the window and stares out at the yard.

"What's the matter, Hoppy?" I ask.

He turns around, and with the bright afternoon sun shining on his back, he looks like a shadow of Abe Lincoln. In a very soft voice, he says, "This is going to stir them up. You got to be careful, David."

CHAPTER 7

The Wrath of the BOP

Mr. O'Connor, my case manager, comes to me with the news that I am being transferred to Sandstone, farther away from Penny. Why? Because I'm having success in court. That's why! Hoppy was right when he said, "They're not going to like seeing you win." I watched as it happened to Norman Flick, another jailhouse lawyer. They put you on the next "smokin' bus" out of here, separate you from your legal papers, and ultimately the court. It's part of the punishment process when the government is incensed at you.

So it's my turn to file an administrative remedy.

Part A: Inmate Request

On April 1990, a progress report was done for transfer, for which I was given a copy of on April 9. The next day, Mr. O'Connor related to me that I will not be considered for Duluth or any other level 1 facility because they were all work camps and I am not medically cleared for work due to my disability. Later, he said he is considering Sandstone, which is not a work camp, and according to him, I no longer need medical treatment. In answer to my cop-out requesting continued medical treatment, Mr. O'Connor's reply was, (a) "You are appropriate for transfer," (b) "You no longer require extensive medical treatment," (c) "You will not be returning to Duluth or any other level 1 facility," (d) "Your request to remain will be rejected," (e) "You are not medically cleared for work," and (f) "Answering copouts takes time away from locating appropriate facility." In response, I filed a BP-9, and nowhere in the BP-9 did I request to be transferred to Oxford or General Population Unit–RCH, as the receipt alleged! I specifically addressed the issue of my disability, the need for medical care, my custody classification, and the hardship on my family. On April 23, Mr. O'Connor, after acknowledging my transfer postponement, claimed that I told him that I couldn't go to Duluth because "I would get into trouble." I did not initiate the transfer, as he implied, nor did I ever say anything about not wanting to go to Duluth. This is a boldfaced prevarication by Mr. O'Connor! I am requesting that no retaliatory action be taken for my raising these issues.

I am not a problem inmate. I have only wanted from the start to be left alone, do my time, and leave through the path of least resistance.

David L. Price
April 30, 1990

I'll have my new attorneys handle it from here, even though they are busy writing my response to the government's reply. They, in turn, hire Marcia Shein, president of National Legal Services, from Atlanta, Georgia. She contacts Mr. J. Michael Quinlan, director; Mr. Geo. C. Wilkerson, regional director; Mr. Ernest Chandler, designations coordinator; the warden; my case manager; and my congress-man, Les Aspin. She writes:

> Please be advised that we have been asked to assist the referenced individual with matters relating to his present custody. A brief history of his circumstances is important to understand the urgency of stopping his pending transfer to Sandstone, Minnesota, and the reconsideration of a more appropriate designation option.
>
> David Price was originally designated to the prison camp in Duluth, Minnesota. He has some severe medical problems, but they did not inhibit his ability to work at the Duluth facility until an accident occurred, which created further injury. David Price broke his back in 1985, and as a result of two back surgeries, he now has wires and rods holding his back together. He was able to function well at Duluth and was teaching courses there. However, after being placed in a top bunk of his sleeping quarters, he injured himself as a result of slipping while attempting to get out of the upper bunk. This slip caused two of the wires holding his back together to break. As a result, a medical evaluation was needed and he was sent to Rochester.
>
> The doctors at the facility in Rochester indicated his injury was severe but that surgery would be dangerous and that if he could stand it, he should wait to pursue further surgery at a later time. Mr. Price is disabled, is walking with a cane, and must be careful in his movement.
>
> Mr. Price is a security level one (1) out custody inmate. At present, he is being told that he will be transferred to a high-security facility, spe-

cifically FCI, Sandstone, as a result of his inability to work. He is being told that being placed at a prison camp would not be an appropriate alternative because of his medical condition. This is obviously an absurd rationale in that PCX Sandstone is a high security level, while Mr. Price is a low-security inmate, and this would be contradictory to BOP policies relating to the appropriate placement of inmates. Not only is Sandstone inappropriate in relation to his security level, but it is also eight hours away from his family, compared to four and a half at Rochester.

An evaluation of this matter, by those in authority to make decisions to effectively save Mr. Price's medical condition from worsening, is necessary to continue his custody time consistent with BOP policy. Mr. Price cannot take a bus ride to Sandstone, Minnesota, without suffering severe problems with his back. This type of transfer would be considered unreasonable if someone carefully reviewed the medical records and asked for recommendations from doctors regarding the risks of such a trip. Additionally, Sandstone is not an appropriate security level facility for this inmate. There is no reason that we can see from a review of BOP policy, that would preclude Mr. Price from being placed at a prison camp facility as originally designated. More importantly, Oxford, Wisconsin, is available to this inmate because it has a work camp as well as an FCI and would be approximately one and a half hours from the family residence. Certainly, Sandstone is completely in opposition to policy statements of the Bureau of Prisons regarding keeping inmates close to home and placing them in security level facilities equal to their rating. In addition, there are other complications that need to be reviewed before sending Mr. Price to Sandstone. Mrs. Price has recently suffered a bout of cancer of the cervix. She was operated on in early 1989 and is expected to recover; however, she is being told that she needs to have limited stress. The stress of driving eight hours to Sandstone to visit her husband is not necessary in this case. More importantly, the stress on Mr. Price as to his medical condition and fear of transfer to a high-security facility also transmits additional stress to Mrs. Price. Additionally, there are BOP alternatives that are more rational and are within policy considerations in placing Mr. Price at a facility other than Sandstone. If the Bureau of Prisons will not keep him at Rochester, where if a medical emergency occurs, he could be treated properly, then he should not be transferred to a facility such as Sandstone when there are alternatives such as the Oxford Prison Camp.

We must be reminded that Mr. Price came from a prison camp and should not be punished for his disability by placing him in a higher-security prison. There are too many issues not being considered in this case consistent with BOP policy. This warrants a review by those in authority to make more rational decisions on behalf of this inmate. He is not asking for any special favor; he is only asking that he be considered for appropriate placement consistent with Bureau of Prison policies and interests. An inmate such as Mr. Price, who has been a model inmate since incarceration, does not need to be punished further. He needs to do his time as peacefully as possible with the support of the prison staff, by placing him in a facility consistent with BOP policies and that would place him close to home in a facility consistent with his security rating.

I request that, upon receipt of this letter, you contact me immediately so we can discuss this matter further. I do not believe anyone wants to see Mr. Price injured further by taking a bus ride to Sandstone, Minnesota, and further by being placed in a security facility that is not consistent with his security rating, his physical condition, or in the interest of justice. He should not be punished for his medical condition. Placing him at a security level facility inconsistent with his status would be unnecessary punishment.

Sincerely,
Marcia Shein
President
National Legal Services Inc.

"Wow! The BOP just got their cheerios shit in!" laughs Garry as I finish reading. The guys love it when I read my legal mail to them.

Hoppy reminds me, "Don't be doing anything wrong. They'd love to put you in the hole."

A few days pass. My "shampoo booze" neighbor asks me, "Do you want to buy some pot?"

I drop my pen in disbelief. "What? Are you kidding?"

"Nope, but it'll cost ya!" he says with confidence.

"How the hell does it get in here? I'm not smokin' something that comes out of some guy's ass!" I say, pretending to be interested. I want to know more. "Do the guards bring it in?"

"No. It's softball pot." And he goes on explaining. "Somebody on the outside takes apart a softball, packs it full of pot, then sews it back up, then drives by at night and tosses it over the fences behind the bleachers at the ball diamond. Early in the morning, it's 'accidentally' stepped into the sand at the horseshoe pit. Later, when the inmates are playing ball, it's picked up and carried back in a softball glove."

"How are you going to smoke it in here without getting caught?" I inquire.

He believes I'm interested, so he proceeds to show me how to make a pipe from a pencil, deck of cards, fingernail clippers, and a piece of scotch tape. First, he takes off the eraser and the eraser holder from a pencil. He digs the eraser out from its brass-colored holder. This becomes the bowl, after he carefully pinches one end. Then a playing card (usually the joker) is rolled up to form a tube and taped. With a fingernail clipper, he snips a little slit and fits the pinched end of the eraser holder into the slit.

He continues explaining, "Put just enough in here for one good hit, take it along with a book of matches, cover removed, that has only one match left to the shower. Smoke it, then dispose everything down the shower's floor drain."

Shaking my head, I say, "I think I'll pass. Thanks, anyway."

These inmates can make contraband out of anything!

Garry says, "Don't believe that softball story. It's the prison's pot, and they're just trying to get you more time. Don't even talk to anyone about doing anything illegal, or you'll be 'ratted out' and charged with 'conspiring' to commit a crime."

Two days later, at 9:00 a.m., the guards enter my cell for a shakedown. Officer Rostad writes me up for an incident report (referred to as a shot) for having in my possession another inmate's property, the legal papers of Malik Muhai Uddin, a man from Pakistan who needed a power of attorney drafted up so his brother, Shair Uddin, could take over and manage his properties. There is no light of freedom at the end of Malik's tunnel. Then they haul me off to take a UA (piss test). I'm tested for alcohol, amphetamines, barbiturates, benzodiazepines, cocaine, opiates, phencyclidine, and tetrahydrocannabinol. All were zero. Not detected.

I fight the shot because, according to the Bureau of Prison's Program Statement 1315, "The warden shall allow an inmate the assistance of another inmate during their leisure time for purposes of legal research and preparation of legal documents."

What are they going to try next? I only want to go home.

That was not where they sent Mike Hunter. He was another jailhouse lawyer who got sent away on the "bus." I hope I hear from him.

I first met Mike in the law library, sitting at a typewriter and pounding the keys with amazing speed. What was even more amazing was, he only used two fingers! He could two-finger-type dictation as fast as you could talk. The man also knew his way around in the law books. I learned a lot from him. His memory for case law citations was incredible too. As he sat in the library, he looked sick. He was way too thin. His cheekbones jutting out from darkened eyes, along with his pale complexion and tobacco-stained fingers, gave him the look of death; however, he had a healthy will in his determination to help anyone who asked.

Mike got to prison by writing to President Reagan complaining about trickle-down economics. His crime was writing down the "thought" that the president should be shot for such thinking.

He represented himself at his trial and ended up in here, the Rochester Federal Medical Center, residing in building 1. This is where the criminally insane are housed, or should I say, "warehoused." Lines of inmates heavily medicated, shuffling their feet as they walk in a zombie-like state from building 1 to the mess hall, were a common sight. But not Mike. He had told me how he would make the best bulimic, especially after being forced to take their "meds." That accounts for his unhealthy appearance, the rotten teeth and all. It was the price Mike had to pay in order to keep his mind. He didn't need or want their drugs, but they would use force. So he filed a lawsuit against the BOP and a Dr. Ruth Westrich, head doctor in charge.

Mike is back in court now. On May 17, 1990, a letter from Mike arrives, written in pencil.

Dear Dave,

Hi! How are ya? I was hoping by now you'd be a free man (with the 2255 motion). I've lost the battle here. I have a hearing scheduled for June 1 that I am not attending. I'm refusing. My expert witness now refuses to testify for me. The judge forcibly appointed a lawyer, whom I have fired. I'm returning. I've had four hearings in two weeks, and each has been hot. One, I was near contempt because I wouldn't sit quietly as the judge asked. He told me the name-calling I've done doesn't effect him. I've since written to remind him people who are worse than baby molesters wouldn't be effected with the truth since they have no conscience and no integrity.

I heard you got a shot for holding someone's legal papers. They're lucky I'm not there. The shot would be illegal/unconstitutional since temporary possession of another's legal papers is essential to functioning as a jailhouse lawyer, for which the government may not interfere, *Johnson v. Avery*, 393 US 483 (1969).

I'm very busy trying to get Chris's lawsuit and appellate brief done. Please help him get the cases I need copied. I will explain later.

"Hunter and Price." Has a good sound to it. We gave them hell, anyway. And it wasn't the staff but lying, snitching inmates who hindered our full blossoming. Are you still being transferred? I hope you know how to go about putting a stop to that (BP-9-10), asserting right to adequate treatment, 503 F.2d 1305; 457 U.S. 307.

How's Garry McClain? I haven't gotten my property yet that is supposedly on its way in the mail.

Dave, let me know how Penny and you are doing, how your Social Security claim is coming, and your court case. Garry can write me, too, if he wants. I would imagine Tommy is gone, isn't he?

I will be there or in North Carolina about the ninth or tenth of June.

I also wish you well. I know I made you mad as hell a few times, but not intentional. Don't worry about me, I'll join Schizophrenics Anonymous. I'm trying to get correspondence with Americans Against Psychiatric Assault (a real organization). Plus others too (Madness Network, for victims of psychiatric hospitalization).

Must close for now.

Your Pal,
Michael "Mad Mike"

The inmates in building 10-1 are mostly older men with ties to organized crime. New York, Chicago, Minneapolis, New Orleans, just to name a few. I don't make it my business to ask why, what, and how come; I just treat everyone the way I would like to be treated. These so-called mobsters are a very likeable bunch. Now, I'm not trying to glorify what any of them might have done or are accused of doing, but what I learn is, they live by the unwritten code: men of honor, loyalty, and trust. They trust me to do their parole hearing appeals, administrative remedies (BP-9s), and cop-outs to the warden. They trust me about drinking hydrogen peroxide, and when one of them was caught with an unauthorized bottle, they were loyal to me and never gave me up in betrayal. They do not snitch!

When Garry and I first knew we had been accepted for a garden plot, I went and told my next-door neighbor, Joe, to consider our garden his garden. "Okay, Sonny," he accepts. I feel it an honor to be growing vegetables for the old man.

I have a perfect view of all the garden plots from my window. One morning, I witness an inmate stealing (imagine that) a not-ready tomato and an unripe pepper from our garden plot. I'm mad. I get out there as fast as I can. I point him out to the "wise guys," and "that is the end of it" is only part of it' honor and respect among thieves, they command.

Baldo Amato doesn't speak English at all. He sits at his garden a lot alongside mine and watches his garden row, too. We come to understand each other. Frank shows me the book *The Octopus*. In the photo section in the middle are Baldo Amato and Salvatore Greco. Baldo was brought to the United States by the Mob to kill (whack) hit men labeled as "out of control." A hit man's hit man. A real-life wise guy. Sal, on the other hand, is a Sicilian "Godfather."

Next to the 10-1 building under the trees are picnic tables, where we all hang out. I'm the only one not speaking Italian. Sal, a tall thin man in his late fifties, early sixties, well-groomed with dark glasses, impeccably dressed, and holding his head high, walks over to our tables. He receives the customary kiss on each cheek that accompanies a Mafia figure of such authority. I'm told that Sal was supposed to be involved with the Pizza Connection, the Sicily-to-New-York heroin ring. Sal's only link to a crime was fifty-five million dollars of unexplained cash in the trunk of his car!

Sal understands English but rarely speaks it. One day I ask Sal, "Do you get your meals in your cell?" (I never see him in the mess hall). He nods. "Do you get extra fruit?" I inquire. Sal shakes his head no. "Do you want extra fruit?" I can't believe I've just asked that—only a doctor can order extra fruit. Sal continues to look a hole right through me. "I'll get you extra fruit," I boast. Sal continues to stare, expressionless, and says nothing.

I've come to know an inmate from India who considers himself as "just a friendly dope dealer." (He's doing ten years for heroin.) He also claims that Manuel Noriega hired his old lawyer. The lawyer who is now wearing his Rolex watch. Anyway, he works in the offices where the computers are. He has previously told me that he can fix the computer to order extra fruit, a commodity that's as good as money. I put him to the test and give him Sal's full name and prison number.

Each day in the yard I greet Sal with, "Extra fruit?" and each day goes by with a shake of the head and a cold, disbelieving stare. One day, I'm working in my garden, tying up tomatoes, when Sal walks up to me and says, "Extra fruit! Thanks." Those are the first and only words of English I hear him say. I can get it done too!

I hope I can get it done for Todd Moeller. My June 16 letter to Minnesota Civil Liberties Union requesting assistance for child abuse states thus:

Dear sir:

I am confined at the Federal Medical Center in Rochester, Minnesota. I am in need of help in a very bad way.

Shortly after my incarceration three years ago, I was divorced. During the divorce, I tried to tell Anoka County that my son was being abused, but they would not listen. So within three days after the divorce hearing, Hennepin County took my son away from my ex-wife because her boyfriend was beating on him.

Hennepin County placed my son in foster care and told my ex that she must complete some programs before she could get him back. They also told her that her boyfriend must not have any contact with our son; however, the strange part is, they let her keep seeing my son and yet told me that I couldn't see him when I did nothing wrong.

In November of last year (1989), I started seeing my son and everything was going along fine. But now my ex-wife has moved back in with that same boyfriend, and I have every reason to believe that my son is in a very dangerous situation.

I am writing to you because I feel my rights as a father were violated and I need your help in protecting the rights of my child, whom I love very much.

My rights were violated by their not letting me see my son, which was stated in the divorce decree, and also by the Hennepin County Public Defenders Office. The lawyer I had from Hennepin County did not even show up at the hearings to represent me!

In short, I need your help to get my son out of the situation he is now in and to help me continue to see my son through this process and afterward.

Enclosed you will find a copy of Hennepin County's finding on the abuse done to my son.

Sincerely yours,
Todd Moeller

Louie has extremely high cholesterol. The medication they prescribe him has yet to be approved by the FDA; instead of getting the recommended dose of thirty milligrams, they give him three hundred milligrams. In a short time after taking it, Louie's eyesight deteriorates to the point he is nearly blind, and when the drug wears off, his sight returns. I sometimes wonder if the government is experimenting on unsuspecting inmate guinea pigs. There would be less lawsuits that way.

Lee Wright is an overweight, friendly, outgoing black man who suffers from diabetes. He is playing cards and, suddenly without warning, collapses to the floor. Louie, who knows CPR, tries to help

Lee, but the guards will not allow it. Instead, they order all of us back to our cells and radio to the medical staff in building 9. They don't arrive for almost *ten minutes*. When they finally do show up (my cell is right next door), Lee is dead. The staff had given him the wrong shot. It seems there are two different types of insulin shots—a fast acting and a much slower release. Lee got too much of the wrong one. Lee died from an overdose of insulin. Oops!

Hoppy is telling Garry and me about his mother, Martha Hopkins, a Knoxville, Tennessee, schoolteacher who loves animals. As a young boy in the Great Depression of the 1930s, Hoppy was surrounded by at least fifteen dogs and too many cats to count. Martha accepted pets that people could no longer afford to feed. Even the strays would find their way to Hoppy's home. One day, Hoppy and his mother were walking past the downtown pet store, and there in the display window was a two-gallon glass water bottle, with its narrow neck, and inside was a full-grown chicken! It couldn't move. Martha was furious. She filed a complaint and took the pet-store owner to court.

The newly formed Associated Press wire service picked up the story as it unfolded in the Knoxville courthouse. The courtroom drama was reported as far away as New York City. The judge reached the bench verdict of not guilty of being cruel to the chicken, because, after all, "it was just a chicken." Martha rose from her seat, grabbed her umbrella upside down, and with its hard maple handle up, swung it like a baseball bat, breaking open the jar sitting on the table. The chicken could only roll and flop. "Your Honor, are you trying to tell us that this is not cruel to this chicken?"

The judge reverses his decision.

Because of the Associated Press and the publicity it brought, a wealthy lady from New York came to Knoxville, and together with Martha Hopkins, they formed an organization known today as the Humane Society. All because of a schoolteacher, a chicken, and a bottle.

There is a very old man living in building 9 whom everyone refers to as Tex. Tex has spent his whole adult life behind bars. Born at the turn of the century, he is known as the last man to rob a train from horseback. He's been in prison since the Great Depression, and word has it, when he finally did get paroled in the 1970s, a Catholic organization tried integrating him back into society. It didn't work. Tex has no family or friends. The things we take for granted were too much for him. He never drove a car.

He never had a job with a paycheck and the responsibilities of paying bills. Tex never used the telephone. He had no one to call. So instead of committing another crime to get back into prison, he went back to the Yankton, South Dakota federal prison and waited outside the walls until the government took him back. Tex has been institutionalized. He will no doubt die in here.

We have a lockdown! Guards suddenly appear from everywhere. On the roofs of all the buildings are armed officers pointing their rifles down at us in the yard. A troop of guards in riot helmets, bulletproof vests, holding billy clubs, jogs in formation to the other side of the yard toward the ball diamond. Nobody moves. This is not an exercise. Somebody is about to be in big trouble. I watch as an inmate from building 1 is apprehended, beaten, handcuffed, put in shackles, and carried facedown, suspended by his handcuffed arms, which are behind his back. It looks painful.

Somebody had thrown a gun over the fence last night. The guards were on top of the situation. They got into position and waited for the inmate to make a move to the gun. I think they know about the softballs, too.

Now we have a shakedown. It's not the same as a lockdown. A *lockdown* is just what it says—all doors to all hallways, building exits, every door, gate, or entry is locked. There is no movement. Everybody freezes until it's over. A *shakedown* means the guards are looking for contraband, which can be anything. Today they are looking for a particular *Playboy* magazine. It seems the guys in building 2 were having Jimmy Bakker autograph Jessica Hahn's tits, and the prison considers that contraband.

I have legal mail today. It's the magistrate's report and recommendation to the Honorable Thomas J. Curran. What if it's bad?

My lawyer's assistant says, "Whatever the magistrate recommends, the government will have ten days to appeal to the district, and if the district court overturns the magistrate's decision, we'll appeal to the Seventh Circuit Court of Appeals, and it'll take till the end of the year at the earliest." She also says, "We need to get out of this without upsetting Boyle. Judges, prosecutors, and lawyers all belong to a bias fraternity. Boyle will take the stand and lie to protect his name—guaranteed."

"Well, that's nice to know. Doesn't anybody care about the truth?" I ask.

"I'm going to call the prosecutor and appeal to his heart versus his vindictiveness. I'll explain that your case was rightly decided by the magistrate," she says in comfort.

"Well, thanks, Janice. It'll be a feather in your cap," I say.

"No. The feather is in your cap, David. It's your case," she says.

I open the magistrate's decision:

> The guidelines were misapplied, resulting in an illegal sentence and ineffective assistance of counsel cause for "procedural default." Now, therefore, it is hereby recommended that the United States district judge enter an order *granting* defendant Price's 2255 motion and that this matter be scheduled for further proceedings in order that the defendant's sentence can be corrected.

I'm starting to cry. I look up and see that I'm not the only one getting emotional. Garry gives me a hug and says, "We're going to miss you, buddy. I'm so happy for you and Ms. Penny."

"I'm still going to keep trying to get you out," I say, reassuring Garry, "and if your judge denies your motion, I'll file an appeal with the Sixth Circuit Court of Appeals."

Hoppy comes over, puts his hand on my shoulder, and says, "You didn't let this place get to you. You've kept your head held high, and you treated everybody with respect. I'm proud to have known you."

"Well, thanks, Hoppy. That means a lot," I say as we shake hands.

I turn back to the magistrate's order and finish reading what the magistrate writes about my request for vocational rehabilitation and, more importantly, what he writes about Odel Gigante, my friend, my neighbor, and my legal representative.

Of course, the government opposes my motion for rehabilitation, and according to them, "the defendant cites no authority for modification of his sentence."

What about *Peeler v. Heckler*, 781 F.2d 649 (Eighth Circuit 1986)? Anyway, the magistrate continues:

> The nature of the submissions filed by the defendant's representative caused the court to make inquiry into that individual's status. According to the records of the Wisconsin Supreme Court, there is no O. R. Gigante who is authorized to practice law in the state of Wisconsin, nor is such an individual authorized to practice in this district court, nor does Mr. Gigante hold himself out as an attorney. An individual may appear in federal court only pro se or through counsel....
>
> With a lay advocate, there is no assurance that the representative's character, knowledge, and training are equal to the responsibilities, nor does the lay advocate have an attorney's ethical responsibilities.

He concludes with, "Consequently, it does not appear that Mr. Gigante may properly make submissions on behalf of defendant Price before this court. Thus, the request for rehabilitation filed on behalf of the defendant should be *denied*, without regard to its merits and without prejudice."

Del is not a "lay advocate." His character, knowledge, and training are above that of so-called lawyers whose ethics are frequently under question. Let's let Del have his say.

> This letter is being submitted on behalf of David Price.
>
> As his agent in Social Security and worker's compensation matters, I wish to bring to your attention that Mr. Price's Social Security benefit has been terminated due to his incarceration. Such termination of benefit is having a serious effect on Mr. Price's terminally ill wife, who is thirty-five years old.
>
> My original motion filed with your court was denied because I am not a lawyer, and one of the main reasoning facts was that I am not governed by the Wisconsin Bar's code of ethics. This is true; however, I am bound by a code of ethics much more complete, that of the Holy Bible. As a Christian, I am trying to reach out for the benefit of my client and his family. The only way I can serve my client, being I am barred from orally submitting my client's position to the court, is by submitting this letter.
>
> Under the Social Security Administration, if the sentencing court orders rehabilitation, my client would regain his benefits for his wife to live on.
>
> I feel the system is barring my client his right to have me come before you because I am not an attorney. I must add, I am highly qualified in administrative law as well as knowing many aspects of civil law, which, at times, affects my area of expertise.

It must be brought to your attention that I have not taken the customary fee that I am entitled to under the Social Security Act when I tried his original case before the Social Security administrative law judge, on which we were successful, and for all the work put into his present Social Security problem. I have taken this position because of the present hardship Mrs. Price and their thirteen-year-old daughter are suffering.

As long as David is incarcerated, without an order for rehabilitation, his family's hardship continues. Therefore, we ask Your Honor for an order for rehabilitation as required under the Social Security Act. I feel there is more at stake here than civil rules of procedure.

Many times attorneys let pride blind them to their true Christian responsibility to the people (their needs) that they represent. We ask that you give this request, which is outlined in my original motion and memorandum in response (attached), that is now incorporated as part of this letter, your serious consideration and favorable response. Your understanding is truly appreciated.

Sincerely yours,
O. R. Gigante

The official order from the judge is issued on my mom's birthday (June 7):

The court will grant the defendant's Section 2255 motion and will conduct a sentencing hearing at 3:00 p.m. on August 8, 1990.

Two guards come to my cell and order me, "Lock up. You're going downtown."

"What's going on?" I ask.

"It's time for your surgery," insists the guard.

"I don't think so. I'm going home in 42 days! I want to call my lawyer," I say, trying not to sound upset.

"Can't do it," says the first guard, acting like a bully.

The second guard asks, "Are you refusing medical treatment?"

Knowing that a refusal to medical treatment puts me on the next smokin' bus out of here, I say again, "I want to talk to my attorney."

They answer in unison, "NO!"

So I sign the medical refusal waiver and make note it's under duress.

What are they going to try next? My lawyer is going to have to deal with the warden and his staff. I quit. If they're doing this just to make me upset, it's working. However, I will remain calm, for a hot temper only lands you in the hole.

The guards come for Hoppy. He is finally going to get to see a district judge. When Hoppy gets to the court, the judge, after reviewing all the paperwork in his file, will not accept his plea of guilty. She says, "Mr. Hopkins, I don't think you are guilty."

Hoppy explains, "Your Honor, they tell me if I plead guilty, they will give me time served."

"But, Mr. Hopkins," insists the judge.

"Your Honor," interrupts Hoppy, "I just want to go home."

It's been four long years since Ms. Kitty and Hoppy have been together. He leaves a lasting impression on all of us. He is my friend forever. Gone, but certainly not forgotten. Neither will Edward W. Smith be forgotten. He was last seen with Jeffery Dahmer.

"Shakedown!" the guard cries out, trying to conceal his delight. Whenever you get a shakedown, they always leave your cell in a mess. This time, with only twenty-five days to go, Officer Daniel Christian (at 11:00 p.m.) writes me a shot for possession of nonhazardous contraband—too many letters (over seven hundred) and too many pictures (over two hundred). He confiscates them. Later, my counselor and I mail all of them back to Penny.

I'm sitting by my garden. It's the best-looking one. My green thumb, along with a little hydrogen peroxide water, have all my plants looking very healthy. Here comes the old man, pushing his wheelchair. He stops and says, "You just keep givin' 'em hell, sonny. We're gonna miss you around here."

"I'm going to miss you guys too," I reply.

"No, you're not. How about a hot pepper?" he asks.

I hand him a jalapeno, and he devours the whole thing and says, "It could be hotter, sonny!"

We both laugh because we know better.

Jimmy Zitnik works for the landscaping department. He comes over, and I can see he is upset. He says, "I need your help."

"Sure, if I can. What's up?"

Jimmy sits down and explains.

He was putting picnic tables out for the visitors that were expected on the Fourth of July. Channel 6 filmed him close up and all for the six o'clock news without his written permission. They didn't have permission from the warden, as they were chased off on two prior occasions by the staff. What they wanted was to get pictures of Jimmy Bakker; instead, they filmed Jimmy Zitnik.

Well, Jimmy's aunt lives nearby and saw her nephew on the news. It was upsetting for the family as well. So I type up a BP-9, and Jimmy files it with the staff. No response. Then I type up a cop-out to the warden. He summons Jimmy to his office. Jimmy is young and scared stiff of the warden. The warden is very friendly toward Jimmy and says he'll retrieve a copy of the tape from Channel 6. Later, Jimmy is called back to the warden's office to view the tape. The scenes of Jimmy are missing (they're spliced out). Thank God there is another tape. Jimmy's aunt, after witnessing her nephew plastered all over the screen from inside the prison walls, records on her VCR the 10:00 p.m. news! Nice try, Warden.

Jimmy recalls how he got busted for cocaine and that he testified against others who are considered dangerous. Some of these powerful people's acquaintances would like to know of Jimmy's whereabouts. Jimmy fears for his life. With him as a protective-custody inmate, his TV appearance has blown his cover. The guards then come to Jimmy

145

and put him on the next smokin' bus out. It's diesel therapy for him. I've never heard from Jimmy again.

The family of Raymond Smith, a.k.a. Ricky Beeks, will never hear from him again but will hear from Jeffery Dahmer.

Garry tries playing softball. As he is running from first to second base, his heart fails and he collapses facedown. I watch as inmates rolling Garry over get shocked with seven hundred volts from his defibrillator. His body jerks violently with each blast. "Come on, Garry, come back!" I scream, hoping he can hear me. After five shocks, he awakens. Boy, that was close! Garry is visibly shaken. His days are numbered, and he cannot get any consideration from the government for his extraordinary physical impairment. His judge thinks he is better off in FMC, Rochester, than at home in Kentucky because of the concern-type treatment he will be getting from the Mayo Clinic. For over a year, his prison doctor thought that bulge and scar in his abdomen was a hernia!

Greg Pope needs help too. He was born in Canada and came to the United States when he was nine months old. From a large family, only he and his mother are not US citizens. He has no ties to Canada. He's lived in the US for thirty-seven years. Immigration has filed a detainer against Greg, and when his cocaine sentence is over with, they will be deporting him to Canada. I type up a request for assistance letter and wish him luck.

I try to help anyone who asks, but I'm running out of time. It's August 3, and the judge excites mail call again with thus:

It is hereby ordered that David L. Price shall be released no later than 10:00 a.m. on August 7, 1990, to the custody of Penny A. Price. This order is specifically directed to the attorney general of the United States, the Federal Bureau of Prisons, and the Federal Medical Center at Rochester, Minnesota. Mr. Price is ordered to appear for resentencing on August 8, 1990, at 3:30 p.m. before this court. The timing of Mr.

Price's return to custody will be determined at the resentencing hearing.

The early morning of August 7, a crowd gathers at the picnic tables outside building 10-1. The guys are having a going-away reception. It's time to say goodbye and good luck before the guards come to take me to receiving. Garry has made me a beautiful three-ring leather folder with bald eagles hand-stamped on the front and back, in flight, about to snag their prey. That, along with the tight double stitching, took a lot of time to make. I shall cherish this forever. I have written a poem to Garry and hand it to him.

I came to prison scared and hurt,
freedom gone and treated like dirt.
I met a man from the Bluegrass State
who showed me that it was wrong to hate.
With a life to live and his body dying,
can't you hear a little girl crying?
"All I want is to be by my dad!"
Why do you want his little girl so sad?
I will always keep trying and always do
whatever I can to help you, too.
Today's goodbye, but it's not the end,
because, Garry McClain, you are my friend.

Tears begin to well up, and when I look at Garry, his eyes are dripping tears onto the picnic table.

Frank comes over and says, "You saved my life. I mean it. You're a prince, I want you to know that. Here is a phone number. If you ever need anything, I mean *anything*, just call."

I give Frank a hug, and my hand can feel the bullet in his back, so I ask, "You sure you don't want the doctors to take this out?"

"Fuck them doctors!" he laughs.

Joe, my cellmate, hands me a sixty-three-page directory of lawyers who sue lawyers and says, "We want you to sue that son-of-a-bitch lawyer of yours. I know you can bite 'em and make it hurt."

I'm beginning to get emotional, and so is everybody else. No matter how tough and hardened one can become like Father Flanigan from Boystown once said, "there is no such thing as a bad boy." Well, today there is no such thing as a bad man. I've given them hope and to never give up.

"Come on, Price, it's time to go," says the guard.

It's a morning with big dark, puffy clouds blocking out the sun, making everything look gray. Then a hole in the clouds appears and a shaft of sunlight beams down just outside the prison gate. There, standing in that spotlight, is Penny, glowing like an angel. She is radiant and smiling, with the biggest stream of tears you'll ever see flowing down her beautiful round little face.

We stand by the car, and my body wraps her sobbing frame. I will never let go of her. I can't let go of her as we sob together. As I look past her toward the prison, Penny comments, "Don't look back, Dave. You're never going to be taken away from me again!"

We drive away listening to Kenny Loggins singing "Celebrate Me Home."

**OBIE'S COBBLESTONE
BAR & RESTAURANT**
East Troy, Wis.

CHAPTER 8

The Resentence

As we leave the the intensive sadness of FMC, the dark clouds continue to rain down their joyous tears, and Penny is doing the same. The Mississippi River soon comes into view, and crossing it back to Wisconsin gives me the feeling of coming home. The thunderheads are retreating behind us, and a rainbow points the way home. What a great day! I'm going home to my family. I've dreamed of this day the moment I first arrived in prison. However, nothing I've visualized has prepared me for the feeling of being unlocked and let go. My arm is out the window, dividing the air like the wing of a bird whose cage is suddenly opened.

We soar into East Troy, floating on the wind of happiness. Penny lands the car behind her father's restaurant, Obie's. As happy as I feel, I can't face the people inside. I climb the back outside stairs over the aroma of frying grease being pushed outside by the kitchen's exhaust fan. I miss that smell.

My emotions are stirring with the joy of homecoming and the fear that tomorrow, at the resentencing hearing, I could be leaving them all over again. I've got till tomorrow. I'm free for now, but not really. I'm staying upstairs in my room, hiding behind a wall of shame. It's easy to do. I've had thirteen and a half months to practice. It's Penny's confidence I now cling to. She tells me, "Dave, when I stood in front of the judge, he looked straight at me. His eyes were concerned and kind, and he asked a lot of questions. I could tell that he is not going to send you back to prison." I recall my lawyer (Janice Rhodes) telling me, "You need to write a long letter to the judge from your heart."

Dear Judge Curran:

My name is David Lawrence Price, and I will be coming before you to be resentenced. I have had many tests and difficulties to overcome in my life, and with the help of God, I have come to see the good.

I was the second eldest of ten children. My parents were lifetime residents of Elkhorn, Wisconsin, and they made their living as dairy farmers. I was raised in rural America on the family farm, a fact that I am very proud of. My father took over the farm from his father, a retired lawyer. I learned at a very young age to appreciate and respect the law.

In high school, I was voted the most athletic, was president of the FFA, and received the National W Award for my achievements in scholastics and sports. I taught my younger brothers and their little friends the art of wrestling, and they all went on to become champions, with my youngest brother a runner-up and champion in the NCAA II. My seven brothers and I are the winningest family in the history of Wisconsin High School wrestling. I know that hard work along with persistence and determination will achieve a goal set.

Fourteen years ago, I married one of the most wonderful women God ever created. Even through our difficult times, Penny and I have had a loving, caring relationship. There has never been a day gone by that we haven't shared together. Thirteen years ago, we were blessed with a child. A daughter who has brought more joy into my life than I could possibly deserve. My life has revolved around my two girls, and every job I ever took was so that I could provide a good life for them.

In 1984, I was diagnosed as having a degenerative disk disease. My life of holding down two jobs, earning over thirty-four thousand dollars a year, which enabled my wife to stay home and be a mother to our daughter, was over. A fact to this day I have trouble accepting. At that time, I refused to admit that there was anything wrong with my back, and I eventually ended up in a wheelchair, unable to work. We suffered through the humiliation of being evicted from our home and moving in with relatives. In March of 1985, I had major surgery as a follow-up to the previous removal of a ruptured disk, which had left me paralyzed. However, they were not able to correct the 50 percent slippage on the L-5 vertebra, so they stabilized it by wiring in a metal bracket and fusing three of my lumbar vertebrae with bone carved from my hip.

The following years of therapy were very difficult both physically and emotionally. The fact that I was no longer able to be the person I grew up as was extremely hard to accept. It was then I became involved with DVR, going to school at Waukesha County Technical Institute in Pewaukee, learning electronics. My grade point for the summer and fall semester was 4.0. However, on the first day of the second semester, on my way to school, my wife and I were in an auto accident that totaled my car and aggravated my back. I could no longer attend school.

My wife now worked two jobs to support our little family to try to keep ahead of the accumulating medical bills that were suffocating us. My parents got back the farm they had sold because the man went bankrupt. They let us move into the house so we could move out of my brother-in-law's home. Being disabled was taking its toll on me. My wife was working, and I wasn't adjusting to the role of Mr. Mom. Many of the duties of the house would throw out my back, like getting the milk out of the refrigerator, pulling down a window shade, vacuuming, putting the dishes away, and making the bed, reminding me constantly when I least expected it that I will never be the same again.

It was at this time, against my better judgment, that I started to drink alcohol. Not a lot at first, but after a while, I began to hide booze around the house and drink at all hours of the day in secret. As a drunkard, I then found it easy to gather the courage to become involved with drugs. By the grace of God and the love of my wife, I entered into Kettle Moraine Hospital on January 8, 1988, and sobered up. Thirty days later, I was released, and I relied on AA to help me accept the fact of who I now was and let go of the anger and stop feeling sorry for myself.

In the following months, I let myself be persuaded into getting involved with growing marijuana. In the following summer months, I had a hard time accepting what I was doing. When my codefendant was arrested, I was frightened and, at the same time, relieved.

At the time of the arrest and subsequent proceedings, my wife, Penny, became very sick. She passed it off as just her nerves (she is a very sensitive person). To this day, I blame myself for her suffering. It wasn't until after my January 12, 1989, sentencing that we learned on February 6 (her birthday) that she had invasive cancer and needed an operation right away. I was given a sixty-day stay by the Honorable Judge Reynolds to be with her when she went through her seven-hour radical surgery to remove the cancer. On the following evening, when she was all alone in her hospital bed, the doctor came to her and explained that the surgery was unsuccessful. The pathologist report stated the presence of cancer in her lymph glands. If she wanted a priest, they'd send one up and leave a sedative with the nurse if she needed it. Our nightmare was only beginning.

Judge Reynolds granted me another sixty-day stay so I could take her to her daily radiation treatments. The doctors have since told her that there is nothing more that can be done for her except regular checkups for the presence of an active tumor and to keep her comfortable with drugs when the end comes.

Your Honor, I love my wife with all my heart! We have always been real close. The pain and suffering that she is going through are more than I can bear. Our little girl has lost her dad to prison, and the fears she has for her mother literally breaks my heart.

On June 21, 1989, I left them and began my prison term in Duluth. The staff there were not the professional caliber you would expect. My disability fell on deaf ears. I was ordered into a top bunk with no ladder to access it and compelled to work. I struggled every day with my back. In order to get into my bunk, I would step on the chair, then onto the top of the desk, and then over to my bed. Because of nerve damage to my bladder from my surgeries, I've always had to go to the bathroom in the middle of the night. In early July, when I was sleeping, someone had inadvertently laid a newspaper on top of the desk for my roommate. That night, around 3:00 a.m., climbing out of bed, I stepped on the newspaper and crashed to the floor. That evening, I was x-rayed and sent back to work at my job as a tutor in the Education Department. The staff would not cooperate, and I remained on the job until my back gave out altogether. I could not straighten up. Finally, an orthopedic surgeon from St. Luke's Hospital, Duluth, was brought in on August 3. He revealed on my x-rays the broken wires and recommended an eight-hour surgery to pin another vertebra and remove the broken wires.

On August 21, 1989, I was sent to FMC, Rochester, for evaluation and treatment. For months, I was being told that they were waiting for my medical records to arrive from Madison. On two separate occasions, I signed release authorizations. April 4, 1990, I was informed of my pending transfer to Sandstone, Minnesota. They said I no longer needed medical treatment. I had my lawyer intervene because I hadn't even been x-rayed, nor had I even seen the orthopedics to be evaluated, let alone treated! Since then, I have had my transfer postponed, I've seen the Mayo orthopedics, and they are recommending a cortisone shot to quiet down the nerve before surgery be done. It appears I have a crack beneath my fusion on the left side.

Your Honor, I have never been in trouble with the law before. I honestly believe I've paid my debt to society. Sir, I am very, very sorry for what I have done, and I accept full responsibility. I have learned a hard and valuable lesson. My wife has suffered greatly, my child has suffered, and I suffer knowing how much they have suffered and still suffer. I want to go home and be a father and a husband. They need me, and I need them. I will persevere to be an honest and productive member of society again.

I appreciate you taking the time to read this letter.

May God bless and be with you.

Respectfully,
David Lawrence Price

* * * * *

Dear Honorable Thomas J. Curran:

I am writing to you in reference regarding *United States v. David L. Price*. On August 8, 1990, Wednesday, at 3:30 p.m., David L. Price will be appearing before you for resentencing. I am the wife of David L. Price. My name is Penny Price. I am thirty-six years old and have been happily married to David for fourteen years. We have a thirteen-year-old daughter named Samantha. Both I and Samantha are patiently waiting for David to return to us. We love him very much.

I would like to have you look at David's real character and put aside the prison number of 02188-089. David is a man with tremendous creative ability. He is a good human being. He is basically an optimistic, confident man. However, in 1985, a dramatic spiral of circumstances changed Dave's personality. He lost his power of being a $35,000-a-year income supporter of our family. He lost control of maintaining his family. He developed a back injury that left him paralyzed and put him in University Hospital, Madison, for two major surgeries. David was no longer able to provide for his family or have things go the way he wanted them to.

We are talking about a man who was always on top of everything and suddenly found himself helpless. He lost his positivity and his desire to communicate. All his ideas and convictions for future happiness were destroyed. When the doctors said he would never work again, he lost his spirit. Keep in mind, we are talking about a born-and-raised Midwestern farmer with eighteen years' wrestling experience and most athletic in all types of competition. It was like his world fell apart and he wasn't accepted anymore. The medical professionals had labeled him disabled. I tell you these things because they are true, not because they are excuses. David was the real working force behind our family, and now that capacity was gone. I was forced to take up two jobs. Dave no longer had that dynamic thrust for living. He was plain out of energy and had no focus for the future. It was right about that time that he found himself at the wrong place at the wrong time. He came in contact with a forty-four-year-old landlord that knew of a way for David to put his feet on a path and stay there until he could once again support his family. I am referring to his conduct in the offense of marijuana plants in a cornfield. I will be the first one to tell you it was a bad mistake. Actually, I will be the second; David would be the first.

David has always had a goal of providing financial independence for our family, and his problem was the way he tried to accomplish it. I would like to point out, in actuality, he *never* did go through with it. When the detectives asked David for his cooperation, he was quick to say, "This is a load off my shoulders." I don't think David would ever have harvested those plants. You see, Judge Curran, David is an honest man. He is not a criminal.

I am trusting your power to open the doors for David and let him return to society. David has come to realize his talent isn't just in the labor market. He has a mind, and with the intelligence God gave him, he can once again take care of the family he so dearly loves.

I am asking you to order time served and let my husband come home to build a future. He is a thirty-eight-year-old man who has painfully paid for his mistakes.

I believe in your power as a judge to see justice take place. Fourteen months of a man's life has been taken away, and those same fourteen months have created a hardship on myself and our daughter that no words can ever express. I respectfully ask for your power to free my husband and Samantha's father.

With sincere regards,
Penny A. Price

Penny, waiting for me to finish reading her letter, returns to her desk and pulls out thirty-three reference letters from people who have taken the time to write to Judge Curran and says, "Janice, our lawyer, told me that we have a judge who will read every one of them."

I put tomorrow's resentencing hearing aside, and for the first time in over a year, I'm back in Penny's arms. I feel like a baby secured by love, and nothing else matters.

Drifting into sleep, I dream of my life growing up on the farm. It was a 160-acre, forty-cow dairy farm that bordered a valley old-timers referred to as Skunk's Misery. Located 4 miles south of East Troy, Wisconsin, the valley held in its belly Sugar Creek. It's a meandering stream flowing east between rows of towering hills covered with sprawling oaks, towering maples, and lush vegetation. When we were young boys, Sugar Creek was our own little Mississippi River, turning us into Huck Finn and Tom Sawyer when we stood in waist-deep water, catching crayfish, fishing with homemade poles, or just floating on makeshift rafts to destiny unknown.

One day in the summer of 1964, playing down by the creek, we discovered three dug holes. They looked like graves, except they were filled with water. When we asked what they were for, the neighbor boy replied, "Dad sold the woods. They're perk tests. Some people from Michigan plan to build a ski resort." The name Skunk's Misery soon gave way to a new name, Alpine Valley.

I smell fresh coffee. Penny let me sleep in. If I have my way, I'll keep sleeping, but it's time to get up and go to Milwaukee and meet with our attorneys, Steve Kravit and Janice Rhodes. They have put together an extremely detailed and thorough, twenty-five-page sentencing memorandum. In it they summarize the facts of my case relevant to resentencing, the law concerning application of the Federal Sentencing Guidelines, and the law concerning downward departures under Sentencing Guidelines section 5H1.4 ("Extraordinary Physical Impairment") and section 5H1.6 ("Family Ties and Responsibilities"). Steve hands me this document and says, "This is what should have been done the first time." It wasn't. The law was completely ignored by my lawyer (Boyle) and the assistant US attorney (Wagner). I wonder, in these times, if the drug area has become a politically reactionary phenomenon in which prosecutors enhance their careers by going for maximum penalties.

We enter into the courtroom with our hopes elevated by our attorney's confidence. The prosecutor doesn't show up. Instead, he sends a young newcomer (Cubbie), whose only concern is cross-examining our expert witness (Dr. Collopy) about whether or not I've received adequate medical treatment from the Justice Department. Judge Curran, after hearing all the testimony, responds, "Downward departure granted. Sentence is reduced to time already served. Probation Department, check to see if he can be released without returning. Upon release from imprisonment, you shall be on supervised release for a term of three years. Case dismissed."

Bang! The gavel hits the desk with the force of a thunderbolt. Penny begins to cry. I turn to thank and shake hands with my two attorneys, and Steve, with a twinkle in his eye, says, "Go home, David."

In Loving Memory Of
Penny A. Price

God saw she was getting tired
And a cure was not to be.
So he put his arms around her
And whispered, "Come with me."
With tearful eyes we watched
her suffer. And saw her fade away.
Although we loved her dearly
it was clear we could not
make her stay.
A golden heart stopped beating
Hard working hand to rest.
God broke our hearts
To prove to us
He only takes the best.

UNITED STATES DISTRICT COURT
EASTERN DISTRICT OF WISCONSIN

DAVID L. PRICE,

Plaintiff,

v.

Case No. 88-CR-115
(Consolidated Civil
Docket Nos. 90-C-0002
90-C-0012)

UNITED STATES OF AMERICA,

Defendant.

ORDER

The court has received the motion of David L. Price pursuant to 28 U.S.C. § 2255 to vacate the sentence imposed by the Honorable John W. Reynolds pursuant to a judgment of conviction on January 12, 1989. Judge Reynolds has recused himself and the case has been randomly reassigned to this court. The court has reviewed the motion and finds that Mr. Price has arguably stated grounds for relief due to ineffective assistance of counsel. The United States Attorney is ordered to file an answer or other pleading within twenty (20) days of the date of this Order.

Done and Ordered in Chambers at the United States Courthouse this _26th_ day of January, 1990.

Thomas J. Curran
United States District Judge

AO 72A
(Rev. 8/82)

David grew up in rural America of the 1950s, helping anyone who would ask. Now, as prisoner of the United States, held in federal custody for growing marijuana, from the prison library, David filed petitions to support his claim of an illegal sentence, and the court agreed. Read what happened to David in prison and the circumstances that took the life of his wife Penny, and the lawsuit that followed. Justice? Or Just Us.

Watched pot never Boyles

Prominent criminal-defense attorney **Gerald P. Boyle** has reached an out-of-court agreement with a convicted marijuana grower who accused Boyle of recommending a plea bargain that brought a prison sentence three times as long as the crime justified. The convict brought a malpractice lawsuit against Boyle that was to have gone to trial in Milwaukee County Circuit Court this week, but the trial was canceled when the parties resolved their differences in an undisclosed settlement. Lawyer **Ronald L. Piette**, who represented Boyle's malpractice says that despite the settlement, "we do not in any way concede any responsibility or liability on the part of Mr. Boyle."

BOYLE

DOCUMENTS ORDERED SEALED

In another development in the lawsuit against Boyle, Reserve Circuit Judge William Moser has ordered key documents in the court file to be sealed from public inspection.

In March, Moser briefly presided over the case before it was assigned to Madden.

Local resident to sue attorney for malpractice

A convicted marijuana grower D

CPSIA information can be obtained
at www.ICGtesting.com
Printed in the USA
LVHW080509100919
630430LV00008B/584/P

9 781645 440451